BOATBUILDING

on

MOUNT DESERT ISLAND

BOATBUILDING
on
MOUNT DESERT ISLAND

LAURIE SCHREIBER

THE
History
PRESS

Published by The History Press
Charleston, SC
www.historypress.net

First published 2016

Manufactured in the United States

ISBN 978.1.46711.868.2

Library of Congress Control Number: 2015955997

CONTENTS

PREFACE

Mount Desert Island (MDI) has a rich history in an astonishing variety of boatbuilding activity, nurtured by families, culture and community. Thanks to the friendliness of everyone I've approached, this project has been a blast and a wonderful education.

My initial focus was traditional wooden boatbuilding from circa 1900 to 1980. At some junctures, I slipped those bounds for no good reason other than that's where my rambles took me. MDI as a center of fiberglass begs a second book.

I am deeply indebted to boatbuilders, families, friends and customers of builders; local history gurus Meredith Hutchins and Ralph Stanley; digital archive wizard Charlotte Morrill; and the following:

- Southwest Harbor Public Library and Digital Archive (SWHPLDA)
- Bass Harbor Memorial Library (BHML)
- Tremont Historical Society (THS)
- Southwest Harbor Historical Society (SWHS)
- Great Harbor Maritime Museum (GHMM)
- Mount Desert Island Historical Society (MDIHS)

Chapter 1

O RICHTOWN BROTHERS, WHERE ART YE?

A SEARCH FOR A BOATBUILDING CLAN

I'm sitting together with wooden boatbuilder Richard Stanley and his wife, Lorraine, in the cockpit of the 1902 Friendship sloop *Westwind*, a multi-year restoration project on jackstands in his shop. The scent of sawdust is in the air. I ask Richard about his influences as a youngster. Richard comes across as a taciturn person at first, but reminiscences get him going.

There was his father, of course, the Southwest Harbor builder Ralph Stanley, who persisted in wood as most other shops took up fiberglass. But Richard said that he learned mainly by watching and by working on the old wooden boats produced by other builders in the areas. There were the brothers Ronald, Roger and Bob Rich and their father, Clifton Rich. Down the road was, and is, the Southwest Boat Corporation, where they'd be tearing the decks off sardine carriers and rebuilding them like new. Bunker and Ellis worked close by, producing high-end yachts and fishing boats. There were the Richtown rollers, made by old Uly and Frank Rich.

I interrupt. The others were familiar names. But who were Uly and Frank Rich? What were the Richtown rollers?

"Ooooh," he says, "they were brothers up on the Richtown Road…When I was young, there were a fair amount of Richtown boats still around, but most of them were on their last legs. They were mostly iron-fastened and pine planks, and the iron just rotted the pine out. But they were well-built boats and not bad looking. When we were kids, my father stored one for Bart

Coffin, who was a lobster bait dealer, and they used it just as a play boat. It was old and tired. I don't know what happened to it."

So it was a while ago. No doubt they were related to the other deeply rooted generations of boatbuilding Riches in Tremont and Southwest Harbor, somehow back in misty time. Their boats, like others of the type, had a tendency to roll side to side. Note to self: Find out more about old Uly and Frank Rich.

HALF A MILE AWAY FROM Richtown and a century ago, Clifton Rich sprang from a different branch of the family and began building boats. He was followed in the craft by his sons, Bobby and twins Roger and Ronald, and by Bobby's son, Chummy. One day, I asked Chummy what he knew about his relatives on Richtown Road, a semicircular village byway that swoops around to Duck Cove and is sometimes just referred to as Richtown.

"Somewhere back along the line, we're all related," he said. "There's that bunch of Riches, there's our bunch of Riches, there's the Riches that own the lobster wharf in Bass Harbor and then there's Jimmy and Merton Rich—all related back somewhere. My mother married a Rich, her sister married a Rich, but two different branches of Riches. So it kind of got confusing."

That's helpful to know but not much. So I give Ralph Stanley a call. The retired boatbuilder spends a lot of time researching the area's maritime history. Frank and Uly, he told me, worked in the 1930s, '40s maybe the '50s. "Their model was quite sharp," said Stanley. "I think the sharpness goes back to when they were building double-enders."

Stanley recalled several Richtown boats, one for Wesley Bracy on Cranberry Island, a thirty-five-footer for Oscar Krantz and others for Frenchboro and Swan's Island fishermen. They built a pleasure boat for one family who hired Tud Bunker to sail it; afterward, it became the Northeast Harbor Fleet's committee boat. The brothers were Jehovah's Witnesses. "If they built you a boat, they'd give you a Bible, too."

Soon enough, I learned that Chummy's cousin Meredith Rich Hutchins is the genealogy guru for the family. She lives in Southwest Harbor, and I made the first of what would be several visits to her home (followed up over many months with lots of e-mails and phone calls, as I took advantage of her wealth of knowledge). An author and former librarian, Hutchins is a font of energy who stores neatly filed masses of documents in her home office. She told me, "Regarding the different branches and their boatbuilding, the boatbuilding Riches of Richtown should include Frank and Ulysses's brothers, Roy and Chauncey."

Ben Hinckley Sr.'s boat *Scamp*. *Everbeck Family Collection.*

Probably *Shearwater*. *Everbeck Family Collection.*

Aha, *four* brothers—valuable information! She also said that, genealogically speaking, she and Chummy descended from a sea captain named Elias Rich Sr. (1779–1867), while the Richtown Riches descended from Elias's older brother, Jonathan Rich (1772–1854). Elias had numerous children, including Elias Jr., who married his cousin, Emily Peters Rich, Jonathan's daughter. I have trouble keeping track, but I guess that's just a taste of Chummy's confusion over the branches that eventually produced him.

Before continuing, it's worth a moment to dwell on Elias *père*, in tribute to his charming place in local lore. He's buried near Bernard, having expired at age eighty-eight. According to Nell Thornton's *Traditions and Records of Southwest Harbor and Somesville*, an exhaustive litany published in 1938 of people's homes and businesses in the locality, Elias, known as "Heavenly Crown" or "Crowny," expressed the hope of "being privileged to wear a crown of glory in the world to come" when he testified at weekly prayer meetings. A discoloration of his gravestone assumed the outline of a crowned head, prompting Holman Day, a Maine journalist and poet of the early twentieth century, to imagine Crowny's nightly prayers:

> *I've never hankered no great on earth for more'n my food and roof,*
> *And all of the meat that I've had to eat was cut near horn or hoof;*
> *But I thank Thee, Lord, that I've earnt my way and I haint got "on the town"*
> *And when I die I know that I shall sartin wear a crown.*

The poem goes on a while, sniping at Elias's wife, who "scoffed" his faith. But now folks "wonder if Elias came from Heaven stealing down/To mutely say in this quaint way that now he wears his crown."

Anyway, remnants of an old Elias Rich wharf can still be seen at low tide on the Richtown shore. It's unclear whether the wharf was built by Elias Sr. or Jr. Meredith mentioned that she heard this from Elizabeth "Dibbie" Parsons, a relation of the Richtown Riches, and noted that I should go and talk with Parsons's sons: Jeff, who works at the hardware store, or Allen, who runs a landscaping business in the heart of Richtown.

By the way, Meredith said, she has a February 15, 1933 *Maine Sunday Telegram* article that discusses the Richtown branch. This was massively exciting. Up until then, I couldn't find any newspaper mentions of the brothers. However, an online search found the rest of the family. The parents were Maurice Peters Rich Jr. and Lois Helen Thurston, born in the 1840s. And there were two more children: Ruthven, called by his middle name, Pearl, was the oldest. Nadia Mae was the only daughter.

The article rightly extols Richtown as a beautiful location where nice people live, mostly self-supporting, and all "rigidly" honest. "No one has ever lived there but Riches and the men and women who have married into the family, and although the young people go away from there to go to sea and to work for a while in the city, usually Boston or thereabouts, most of them eventually come home."

The text notes that the first Rich arrived in the area by boat, necessarily, from Marblehead, Massachusetts. "His name was Jonathan and his equipment consisted of his young wife, a pair of oxen and one very strong hand, the other hand having been lost in some accident or battle forgotten in the shades of history."

Jonathan selected a location where there was good soil, a freshwater stream and a shelving beach suitable for shipways to launch vessels into beautiful Blue Hill Bay. This was the start of generations of Riches building clipper ships, coasters, fishing boats and yachts. For the time, Jonathan's son, Maurice Peters Rich Sr. (1805–1879), was the most famous builder of the family; his activities coincided with the clipper ship era of American history. Some of his better-known vessels were the *Seabird*, the *Tangent* and the 150-foot, three-hundred-ton half-brig *M.P. Rich*. Anecdotes about Maurice commemorate his individualism. One day, he capsized in a gale. He crawled up and straddled the keel, in danger of being swept off in the heavy seas. A rescue boat arrived.

"Can you tow in the sloop?" yelled Maurice.

"No," came the reply. "I can save you, but I can't tow your boat."

"All right," said Maurice, "I'll ride my wooden horse until somebody comes along who can tow her."

Rich-built boats, the writer noted, are solid and long-lasting. At the dawn of the twentieth century, the clan accommodated the arrival of the gasoline

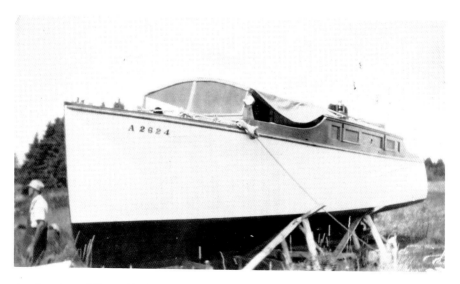

Another view of *Scamp*. *Everbeck Family Collection*.

engine by designing a new craft suitable for fishing offshore throughout the year and capable of fair speed. Richtown and Clifton Rich boats dominated fishing boat design in the area. "No Rich has ever built a boat that couldn't work off this shore all winter, and probably couldn't be hired to do so."

By then, the brothers, averaging thirty years old, had developed a compound of about eight houses. When the article was written, they were building a boat for a local fisherman. Their work was coveted by recreational boaters, too. Among them were the wealthy and prominent, such as Richard C. Paine of Paine and Webber in Boston and Ernest Martin Hopkins, Dartmouth College's president from 1916 to 1945.

SOON IT WAS SPRINGTIME, and Parsons landscaping trucks appeared around town, reminding me to go to the hardware store to buy grass seed. This put me within aisle space of Jeff Parsons. I asked him how his mother, Elizabeth Parsons, was doing and if she knew the Richtown Riches. Oh my goodness, yes. Jeff himself remembered Uncle Frank. I should give his mother a call.

At the seaward bulge of the Richtown peninsula, greenswards roll down to the shore, dotted by homes and rental cottages. Elizabeth's house is at the center of this neighborly cluster. I didn't have a good handle yet on how she's related to the Riches. She took me inside and showed me a photo of her late husband, Allen Parsons Sr. Allen's mother was Mae, the sister of the boatbuilding brothers and the owner of the house in which Elizabeth lives. Elizabeth pointed out the kitchen window to a white house with black shutters. That was Uncle Frank's house. Uncle Uly lived in the white house next to that. Roy had another house behind the trees. Chauncey died before Elizabeth was married to Allen. Also seen is a barn-like structure. That's where the boatbuilding shop was.

Elizabeth explained that Frank was married to Goldie Corinne Thurston. Goldie ran a summer tearoom in her house. Goldie's sister was Georgia, whose nickname was Sally. The sisters were close, and Goldie and Frank, who never had children, absorbed Georgia; her husband, Charles Reed; and their seven children into their family life. Georgia's younger daughter, Virginia Everbeck, inherited Frank and Goldie's house. Therefore, thought Elizabeth, the Everbeck family might also have inherited the old boatbuilding records. Also, Betty Wass, who lives across the street, is the granddaughter of one of the Rich brothers—although she's not sure which one—and she might remember things.

But Elizabeth does have a half-model of one of the brothers' designs. Allen Sr. inherited it, and it's mounted on the wall of a rental cottage owned by

Standing, left to right: Chauncey, Uly, Frank and Pearl. *Seated, left to right*: Lois, Mae and Roy. *Everbeck Family Collection.*

Allen Jr. "I could show you that, because it's not rented right now," Elizabeth said. We made the short drive across Richtown Road to the cottage. High on the wall hangs the half-model, in dark varnished wood. I feel a thrill. It's like a treasure hunt. I should give Mrs. Everbeck and Mrs. Wass a call.

"I can remember the big doings when they would launch a boat. The lady would crack the bottle of champagne on the bow, people would appear and we all had to be on our best behavior," said Winifred Howie. Virginia Everbeck (who passed away after this writing) had deputized her oldest daughter, Winnie, to talk with me.

Winnie's father, LeRoy "Roy" Everbeck, was a radioman in the South Pacific during World War II and then worked for the brothers for several years. Winnie remembered the boatbuilding operation as a young child in the 1940s. She took me back a few generations. Maurice Peters Rich Sr., the builder of clipper ships, had a son named Maurice Peters Rich Jr., who became a carpenter. Maurice Jr. married a local lass, Lois Thurston, and they moved to Lynn, Massachusetts, and had six children. Ulysses gained

The *Marilyn* being launched. *Everbeck Family Collection.*

renown as a pitcher and first baseman for the Lynn ball team and was viewed as potential major-league material. But in 1892, at age fifty-one, Maurice was killed, possibly when some timber fell on him. Pearl was twenty-one, Roy nineteen, Chauncey seventeen, Ulysses fifteen, Mae thirteen and Frank eleven. Lois's only recourse was to move her brood back to Tremont. Her father's family, the Thurstons, gave her a large parcel of land. This might be when the area acquired the name Richtown, as her married name was Rich.

At first, two or three of the older children stayed in Lynn. When Frank grew to adulthood, he and Chauncey started to build boats, although there's some thought that Ulysses was the brains behind the operation. Eventually, Roy joined them. Pearl was born with an abnormality in his hands, so he was limited in his work.

Frank fell in love with Goldie Thurston, the granddaughter of Lois's older brother Solomon and, therefore, his cousin once removed. Goldie was in Massachusetts to care for her invalid mother, so in 1910 Frank went down and they eloped. Goldie stayed in Massachusetts, and Frank returned to Richtown to work on boats and build a tiny house for his bride. "And this is the house we're in now," said Winnie.

They had a commuting marriage the first year or two, with Frank catching the steamboat in Southwest Harbor to travel to Boston. When Goldie finally joined him, she helped run the office side of the boatbuilding business.

A family cow. *Everbeck Family Collection.*

An unidentified pleasure boat. *Everbeck Family Collection.*

Everyone worked hard. The large, cedar-shingled shop attached to the barn had a two-story interior and a block-lettered sign that read, "Rich Bros Boat Builders." It was surrounded by hayfields and farmland. The family kept cows, a horse, chickens, doves, carrier pigeons and pigs. "I remember the bull in the yard. That was an adventure," said Winnie. "There was a whole self-supporting little ecosystem."

A horse-drawn boat launch. *Everbeck Family Collection.*

The brothers got their business mostly by word of mouth, mostly from local fishermen and summer residents, building mostly one boat per year. Frank kept and cherished the postcards sent by customers as they sailed the seas in their boats. "Frank was definitely old-school," said Winnie, who recalled the little curls of wood that emerged as the men planed the planks; the big, soft mallet her dad used when he bunged the screw holes; the application of coat after coat of varnish on the mahogany; the "pinky peachy orange" color of the painted hulls; and the finished boats rolled on logs, towed by a horse, down the hill to the shore to be launched.

The summer scene was lively. Thurston and Reed family members from away visited as much as possible, and various relations by blood and marriage built summer camps and rental cottages. In the late 1930s, Goldie operated from her home the summertime Lighthouse Tea Room, overlooking the water. Distinguished guests jaunted in by horse and carriage to sit on the lawn and enjoy the view and company. "Aunt Goldie was quite the cook. She served homemade popovers, pies, blueberry cake, tea and real lemonade," Winnie noted.

Frank crafted a miniature lighthouse and little houses for her to decorate the grounds. Goldie put on baked bean suppers every Saturday night. The children helped feed the animals and grade eggs. Winnie and her cousin Marie climbed up on the roof of the boat shop to listen to the Boston disc

Goldie. *Everbeck Family Collection.*

jockey Arnie "Woo Woo" Ginsburg on the radio. The clan played baseball in the field. "They let everybody hit, even the little kids," said Winnie.

I jaunt across the street to Betty Wass, who also remembered such doings. It turned out that she's Uly's granddaughter. He was irrepressible. "He would disagree with you about everything, no matter what," she said, rapping the table. "To get an argument going—that was his main thing. He was good though, Grandfather was. He wasn't the kind who thought he knew everything."

Life could be rough, she said, but they weren't rough men. They never drank; everything was aboveboard and honest. Family was paramount. "They all had to work hard to get by. Uncle Frank told me they would cut wood down to Seawall [miles away]. They had to walk down every morning. They had to use a lantern to find their way down, come home after dark. You don't see too many now that would be doing that."

The boatbuilding came to an end through natural causes. Chauncey died in 1939 at age sixty-four. Roy died in 1944 at age seventy-one. (Mae had died in 1935 at age fifty-six.) Betty recalled her grandfather's death: "There was a well between this house and that house, and he was carrying water over the road to his grandson's and he just dropped dead. Set down two buckets of water and just died." That was in 1951 at age seventy-four. "When my grandfather died, Uncle Frank couldn't get anyone from the family, I think, to help him build boats, so that was the end of it," she said.

Mr. Dunbar's boat launch, August 17, 1951. *Everbeck Family Collection.*

After the business closed, Frank occupied himself with wood-carving, making model boats and lighthouses. A Massachusetts restaurant called the Ship (in the shape of a big ship on Route 1 in Lynnfield) commissioned him to build a practically life-size lighthouse.

Goldie's death in 1966 at age seventy-seven left him bereft. He lived by himself for a while, with folks checking in on him. He had a strong friendship with Goldie's sister, Georgia Reed, whose husband, Charles, had died. For the next decade, Frank lived winters with Georgia and her family at her home in Winthrop, Massachusetts. Nieces and nephews remembered him sitting in the kitchen corner telling jokes and pranking. He returned to Richtown each summer. In 1976, at Georgia's house, he died at age ninety-two. He is buried next to Goldie in the family cemetery in Richtown, along with his parents and most of the Rich brothers boatbuilders.

I MADE MY LAST CALL to Lillian Hodgdon, not knowing what to expect except that she's Betty Wass's sister and might have more material related to Uly. At her home in Bernard, Lillian, a welcoming person, is intrigued by the idea of teasing out stories from bits of information scattered in attics and memories. She showed me vintage portraits of a young woman. This might be Uly's wife, who died young. Then there's gold—Uly as a youth in his baseball uniform, a good-looking lad.

I asked what she remembered about her grandfather, whom she called Gampa. "Oh, he was a moderate soul. I think the Riches, most of them were." She laughed with pleasure. "He was a good gentleman, my grandfather was."

We chatted about home and relatives, old photos and stories. She racked her brain to see if she could remember more about the brothers, wishing she had thought to write things down over the years. But it's too long past. Memories almost come, but she can't quite grab them. "You forget this stuff. It goes for ages, then all of a sudden it just drifts away."

Chapter 2

A RICH HERITAGE

"ALL I WANTED TO DO WAS BUILD BOATS"

I built boats from the time I could walk," said Robert "Chummy" Rich. "Most of them wouldn't float. If they did, they'd float upside down."

When Rich was a kid, he liked nothing better than to hang out with his grandfather, locally renowned boatbuilder Clifton Rich. He borrowed scraps of lumber from his dad, Robert "Bobby" Rich, also a well-known builder. Sometimes, young Rich got into the good stuff. By the time he was ten or so, he'd put together a pretty good-sized craft. In a vintage photo, he and his buddies Ralph Tate and Morris Thurston from up the road can be seen clambering into it as they ease it into the water.

"You had to bail quite consistently, but it did float," he said. "The only means of propulsion was—you're on the boat, you throw the anchor out as far as you could throw it, you haul yourself along and then throw it out again."

Coming from a long line of boatbuilders, shipbuilders, seafarers and carpenters, and enjoying tutelage from a network of family members and their skilled employees, Rich had no trouble from then on making his boats float and establishing his own reputation as a builder of fine craft.

On the "back side" of Mount Desert Island, in the adjacent coastal towns of Tremont and Southwest Harbor, the Rich clan "goes all the way back to Noah," Chummy joked, adding, "We have built just about everything."

The Clifton, Bobby and Chummy branch of the family produced at least 367 boats in an astonishing variety. In the early twentieth century, Clifton's punts, dories, small fishing boats and sailboats were mainstays for the local fleet. When Bobby started his shop in 1939, he became the go-to builder for

Young Chummy (right) with pals, put in their scrapwood vessel. *Robert C. Rich Collection.*

all manner of work boats, recreational boats and specialty craft; his boats sold from Maine to South America.

Chummy began working in his father's shop in 1958 and took over operations upon his father's death in 1981. Backed by ten generations in the local dynasty, his name is something of an institution around the harbor. "That's 'mental' institution," he quipped.

WHEN YOU GET TO talking about the Rich clan, you have to shift to nicknames, as there's a fair bucketload of Johns, Jonathans and Samuels through the ages. There was "Lyin' Sam," "Sam Peculiar" and "One-Wing Sam," who lost an arm in the Civil War. There was "Devil Sam," "Devil John," "Dum-a-Diddle John," and "Gorry John," named after his favorite curse word, *gorry*. Gorry John married a twelve-year-old when he was twenty-five and never made a decision without asking her. "Well, gorry now, I'll have to ask Mar," he'd say, according to Lillian Rich Reed, recorded in a January 16, 1967 interview conducted by the Mount Desert Island Historical Society (MDIHS).

"Talking John" Rich with wife, Charlotte Rich, and family, circa 1909–12. *Eleanor R. Mayo Collection/SWHPLDA.*

My favorite nickname is "Talking John." One day, I return to Meredith for explications. "Why was he called Talking John?" I asked her, apparently brain-dead that moment.

"I suppose he talked a lot," she charitably answered. "And my grandfather was very talkative. And my father was very talkative. In fact, I think we all talk, given the opportunity."

According to Meredith, the first of the antique Riches to arrive in Tremont, around the time of the American Revolution, was a Grand Banks fisherman named John. "He used to boast that he had eaten sixteen Christmas dinners on the Banks," as noted by William Otis Sawtelle in *Bangor Historical Magazine.*

John fathered a large family, including Elias "Heavenly Crown." Heavenly Crown had twelve children, including Elias Jr., whose children included Talking John. Talking John was master of a number of vessels. He married a local lass, Charlotte Kelley. Their first child, Orville, died at age two when he drowned in a spring. A year later, they had Clifton, followed by three more children.

From a young age, Clifton went to sea with his father and probably helped him build the family homesteads, as well as the local store and a church. Cliff's teenage years weren't all work. With siblings and friends, he spent evenings in the local dance hall. At the library, they played tiddlywinks and checkers, as Lillian Rich Reed in 1967 and Emily Rich Trask in 1975 noted via MDIHS.

Cliff once told Meredith's brother that as a young man on a trip on the schooner *Idaho*, he was caulking the deck while the vessel was tied up to a Boston wharf. "A man came by and watched him work and then said to Cliff, 'A man's a fool to go to sea when he can caulk like that.' 'And you know, he was right,' Cliff said, so he came home and began to carpenter and build boats. He didn't want to go to sea anyway. He said, 'It was dangerous, the food was bad and it was a hard life,'" according to Meredith Rich Hutchins via the Tremont Historical Society (THS).

Cliff built a house and small shop in Bernard and probably got his first boat commission in about 1910. One reporter called Cliff the "Wizard of Bernard Corner," a tribute to his "Bass Harbor" lobsterboat designs, considered faster than others. An old clipping tells of a thirty-footer he was building: "This boat follows the same design as that recently completed in the Rich shop for Earl Awalt, Frenchboro lobster fisherman. Awalt's boat

Cliff Rich and Eddie Hamblen build a punt, 1949. *W.H. Ballard photo/Robert C. Rich Collection.*

has a Chrysler Crown straight drive, and is said here to make the run from Long Island to Bass Harbor in less time than any other Frenchboro boat."

One of Cliff's bigger dories, and the oldest of his boats still in existence, is probably a twenty-footer that served Nan and Art Kellam. The couple lived nearly four decades on Placentia Island, two miles off Bernard. Art was a World War II–era aeronautical engineer. In 1949, they bought the island to live a life of seclusion and self-sufficiency and needed the boat to carry supplies. At various times, the *BLB* (for "Bear loves Beum," their nicknames for each other) carried "furniture; a cook stove; a shower stall; and an array of material for Homewood's construction, including windows, lumber, pinewood paneling for the interior, and shingles for the roof," as noted by Peter P. Blanchard III in *We Were an Island: The Maine Life of Art and Nan Kellam.*

Cliff and his wife, Elizabeth, had four children—twins Roger and Ronald, Bobby and their youngest, Cecil, who died at age fifteen from leukemia.

Meredith recalled her teenage uncle in a THS newsletter: "I was two and a half years old at the time and can remember seeing him shortly before his death lying in a hammock on the porch at my grandparents' house with a basket of fall apples nearby."

A 1920s clipping commends young Robert, Ronald and Roger as "Expert Boat Builders." A photo shows two of the boys, age thirteen and fourteen, with some of their models, including a two-masted schooner, a powerboat with the trysail on the stern and a Marconi-rigged sloop. The author admires the "marvelously correct design and good workmanship…They sometimes power their motorboats with works from an old eight-day clock, gear wheels being removed so that the machinery can expand its eight days' energy in a few minutes."

In 1939, Bobby bought property on the Bernard shore, a lovely ramble down from his parents' home, and built a small shop. When World War II came along, he became foreman at the Southwest Boat Corporation, building navy vessels. Afterward, he returned to his business, called it the Bass Harbor Boat Company and soon expanded to two main buildings and three marine railways. His first projects were small lobsterboats, but soon he was building good-sized pleasure boats for an expanding clientele. At the time of his death, he had built at least 165 commercial and recreational boats. The variety is phenomenal—seiners, luxury cruisers and motor sailers, lobsterboats, sportfishermen, tenders, towboats, research vessels, utility boats and police boats.

Bobby Rich's shop, late 1940s or early 1950s. *Tremont Historical Society.*

Probably the oldest still in existence is the fifty-foot dragger *Bajupa*, built in the late 1940s for the Rackliff and Witham Lobster Company in Rockland. The biggest boat might have been the fifty-seven-foot motor sailer *Lazy Lady*, a John Alden design launched around the early 1960s for an Arlington, Massachusetts family. Its dinghy was named *Tired Miss*. The owners wanted the cockpit dolled up with teak Formica. That posed a problem. "We put it out in the sun, and it just fell off," Chummy recalled. "It got so hot the glue let go. We put Formica down in the cabin—not a problem. But outdoors, with the sun beating on it, we had to tear it all off and do it over again."

Launching parties were quite the event, drawing scores of people. "People got dressed up, and a lot of the local fishermen ended up at the parties—free booze," Chummy noted.

Morning Star had rather a "podauger" (old-fashioned) look about it, Bernard resident Malcolm MacDuffie wrote about the thirty-foot cabin cruiser Bobby built in the 1950s. That's just what MacDuffie wanted. The Monterey-style yacht, designed by William Garden of Seattle, was his "personality boat," combining the lifting qualities of the Friendship sloop, the easy-driving ways of the old peapod stern and the four punt-loads of beach rock for ballast.

There's the John Alden–designed luxury yacht *Whitecap*, built for Gordon and Robert White of Boston, owners of the nautical instrument firm of Wilfred O. White and Sons. Unsurprisingly, the new boat was well equipped

Bobby Rich launched *Fantee*, a twenty-six-foot yacht for a Boston doctor, in 1958. *W.H. Ballard photo/Robert C. Rich Collection.*

with navigation instruments. It wasn't as yachty as *Lazy Lady* but was still fancy enough to get into *Yachting* magazine.

Most sales were by word of mouth. Jeanne St. Andre Merkel and her husband, longtime live-aboard cruisers, were looking for a Brooklin boat shop when a passerby told them to go see Bobby Rich instead, saying, "He's the best boatbuilder and man you could hope to find!" as noted in *Nine Boats and Nine Kids*, written by Merkel. Bobby built them the cruiser *Lady Jeanne* and ended up a close friend.

Many other boats highlighted the simplicity and elegance that were attracting pleasure boaters to the "lobsteryacht" concept and fishermen to Bobby Rich's rugged designs. A handsome yacht built along lobsterboat lines was named *Tim Tam* after the owner's Triple Crown racehorse. The design inspired *Danielle*, a beautiful running hull that still fishes out of Bass Harbor. *Danielle* was recently overhauled and still looks brand new inside.

From 1950, Bobby had a key friend in George Davis, general manager (and later owner) of Plymouth Marine Railways in Duxbury, Massachusetts. Davis had his own boat built by the Rich yard, hooked

Tim Tam. Robert C. Rich Collection.

Bobby up to build boats for the Massachusetts Law Enforcement Division and turned commercial and sport fishermen onto the Rich brand. One newspaper reckoned that the sleek forty-seven-foot offshore lobsterboat built for the Cape Lobster Company of Hyannis, Massachusetts, would "give some competition" to the Soviet fishing fleet that was plying the North Atlantic's state waters at the time. In Green Harbor, Massachusetts, sales took off. "I think it was thirteen out of twenty-one full-time fishermen had boats that we built," Chummy recalled. "Every time we built a new boat for somebody down there, all the other fellows would show up at the launching."

Through Davis, Bobby contracted with the Plimoth Plantation living history museum in Massachusetts to build a seventeenth-century replica "shallop" of the style that traveled with the *Mayflower*. Bobby supplied materials and sent his brother Roger and Roger's good friend Mickey Fahey to do the work. A report from the day notes that the Maine company was selected because no Massachusetts craftsmen were skilled enough in the handling of wood tools to build it.

Bobby Rich, Garry Moore and *Little Toot*. *Robert C. Rich Collection.*

Bobby gained national renown for his "baby tugboat" design, which he called *Little Toot*. He built the eighteen-foot miniature tugboat in 1959 as a spare-time project. With scooter-tire bumpers and a black smokestack, "Little Toot resembles a Disneyland creation with bright red super structure, green hull and white trim," as a clipping relates.

Bobby used the boat for fun and for small-boat work. The distinctive craft attracted the attention of nearby resident Garry Moore, who was a well-known yachtsman and a prominent television personality (host of *I've Got a Secret* and *To Tell the Truth*) and who had a summer home in Seal Cove. Moore made an offer Bobby couldn't refuse. *Little Toot* was a beloved sight wherever Moore went, especially Hilton Head Island, South Carolina, where Moore retired in the 1980s. The tug "brought big smiles to a lot of people on the island," wrote reporter David Lauderdale in the *Island Packet* in 2003.

Bobby built four or five mini-tugs. The producers of the television game show *The Price Is Right* bought one to give away as a prize. A $4,000 bid won the boat. Another, *Fran's Folly*, was outfitted with a stack belching "real, although unnecessary, smoke puffs." A mock scanner was fashioned from a car's windshield wiper mechanism and mounted atop the pilothouse, as were three canned-air horns. "One of these blasts out a low throaty Tooot!" as the *Post-Times* in Florida noted in 1968.

CHUMMY FONDLY REMEMBERED spending time at both his father's and grandfather's shops as a kid. "Just kind of underfoot, making a nuisance of myself," he said.

He had his first professional commission at age fifteen when he built a sixteen-foot inboard powerboat for local fisherman Sheldon Smith during the winter of 1955–56. "It was built nights and weekends, with considerable amount of help from Father and some of his crew," he said. "For the time, it was a bulky sixteen feet. It was difficult to build because it was so full forward. But it was a real stable boat and worked out just great for fishing and towing dories."

When Chummy graduated from high school, he did a summer stint at the nearby Hinckley yard, which was making a name for itself in high-end yachts. But his temperament was not quite right for the yard's "rules and regulations." The yard was building a sixty-foot wooden yacht, and the owner wanted Chummy to go deckhand. "We had a little meeting, and the captain said, 'I'm going to explain your duties to you. You'll have to wait on tables and do laundry and dishes and serve cocktails.' Well, that's not what I signed up for. That basically ended it."

He returned to his father's shop, working with Eugcnc Walls, his father's compatriot and Chummy's mentor. "Father was there and he'd make all the decisions, but Eugene taught me what size drill to use." By the time his father died, the wooden boat business was fading away in favor of fiberglass. Chummy wasn't interested, so he mainly focused on producing wood finishes for fiberglass boats, on storage and maintenance and on his boat transportation business. In the early 2000s, he thought he'd retire all together from the craft and concentrate on boat transportation.

Instead, a younger wooden boat enthusiast, Richard Helmke, landed on his doorstep. When he was thirteen, working at a boatyard in Nyack, New York, Helmke came to know a wooden boat named *Spoiler*. He loved its traditional style, shapely and narrow. Years later, he bought it, tracked down the original owner and discovered that it was a Bobby Rich boat, built in 1959. *Spoiler* was in pretty good shape but needed repairs. One day, he called Chummy for advice on its restoration and then traveled up for a visit. The two men hit it off.

Helmke recalled a discussion they had one night at dinner. "He indicated how he'd love to retire and sell the place, but he'd miss it. And that's when we came up with an idea together: What if I bought the place, you still keep coming in and do your thing every day and enjoy it as long as you want— and it works out great for both of us?"

The Bobby Rich boat that won Rich Helmke's heart. *Richard Helmke.*

The idea took. Helmke moved his family from New York to Bernard and bought the place, while Chummy kept his own schedule. The two men, with Chummy's longtime right-hand man, Bobby Kelley, were soon building the first wooden boat to come out of the shop in twenty-five years, a twenty-eight-foot carvel-planked cabin-cruiser based on *Spoiler*'s design. "Chum's built so many boats in his life, it's just [Helmke snapped his fingers to indicate autopilot] like that. Where we sort of have to stand back and think about it, he knows exactly where to go."

"You've got to want to do it," said Chummy. "Especially to stay at it as long as we Riches have. When I was six years old, I was down on the beach with a board and a nail in it and a string on it, pulling it around and playing boat. I've always done it and always liked it and found a way to eke out a living—and have fun, too."

Chapter 3

RICH & GRINDLE

"LET'S GO BUILD A BOAT IN MY BARN"

Roger Rich and his friend Ralph Grindle founded Rich & Grindle Boatbuilders in 1946, building boats in Rich's barn at Tracy Cove on Clark Point Road in Southwest Harbor. The two men were in their early thirties and had been working for Henry Hinckley, who had major boatbuilding contracts with the military during World War II. After the war, the story goes, Rich and Hinckley had a falling out, so Rich persuaded Grindle that it was time to leave and start a new operation.

Their timing was excellent. Servicemen were returning to the Maine coast after the war, had money and wanted new boats. Roger's brother Bobby had more work than he could handle. Bobby farmed out a contract to the newly established Rich & Grindle to build a thirty-two-foot lobsterboat for Vernon Dalzell of Frenchboro for $2,500. That first boat, the *Eva G.*, hit the water the following year.

Soon, the shop was plenty busy. There were slack times, sure, when the two took carpentry jobs and, at one point, laid linoleum. But orders kept coming, both from high-end yachters and fishermen.

"Rog is a conundrum," his Pemetic High School yearbook notes. "You never know in what mood you're going to find him, for his temper is as changeable as the weather. However, we can't help liking him and no matter how angry he makes us, we always have to forgive him."

Inevitably, I returned to Meredith, who is Roger's daughter. She said that her dad probably "raised hell" in high school. At her home, Hutchins turned

Bobby and Ronald (second and third from left) and Roger (right) with *Kada II* at Bobby's shorefront shop, 1942. *Robert C. Rich Collection.*

to page ten in the 1931 yearbook, where headshots show her twin uncles as teens, Ronald in a bowtie and her father in round spectacles. Both wear a slight smile. The boys are pigeonholed under the heading of "commercial" rather than "college."

The Great Depression was on when the twins graduated. Jobs were few. One summer, Roger, Ronald and Bobby drew straws to see who would go to the local unit of the Civilian Conservation Corps, the federal public work relief program. Roger got the short straw. "With no work available, the thirty dollars a month the government paid the men's families made the difference between independence and going on the town," according to Meredith via the THS newsletter.

Roger hoped to do carpentry work but was assigned to dig out stumps and ended up mostly doing KP duty and peeling potatoes because he was always in trouble. He got out as soon as he could and did a lot of different things. He cooked for a local logging operation. In the late 1930s, he opened a gasoline station on the corner below his parents' house. The business was not successful. "When I asked my father why not, he said it was probably because he accepted too many bushels of apples as payment for gas, a practice that couldn't have helped his cash flow, especially during the depression," Hutchins wrote. "Everybody did his best though, including my mother, who made fudge to sell there, and Mr. Roscoe Ingalls, Tremont summer resident, who liked to use high-test gasoline in his automobile and would buy an entire tankful at the beginning of the season, so it would be available whenever he wanted it."

Roger worked for Bobby early on, for Hollis Reed (his uncle by marriage) at the general store and during the war for Hinckley and Bink Sargent at Southwest Boat.

RALPH GRINDLE, BORN IN 1915, grew up on Deer Isle, thanks to the work his father found there cutting the world-famous pink-gray granite at quarries in the surrounding area.

During the Depression, Grindle was a teenager going to high school in Stonington and working for the CCC in Southwest Harbor during the summer. Unlike Rich, he loved the camp. "He told me that he just loved hanging out with the men," said Grindle's daughter, RuthAnn "Sugar" Fenton, who lives in Lamoine. "They treated him well. He ran errands for them and did minor chores."

Ralph and Ruth Grindle at their house, 1946. *RuthAnn Fenton Collection.*

Grindle arrived each summer on the steamer *J.T. Morse* and stayed with relatives. He worked in the woods, drove a park truck and was promoted to tool clerk. Grindle went on to serve in the U.S. Navy during World War II, stationed in the Hawaiian Islands. When he returned, he took a job with Hinckley in the tool department and then became foreman of the spar shop, in charge of splicing and rigging. Rich came on a bit later and would soon call Grindle one of the best wire splicers in the business. Grindle shared with Rich the traditional mnemonic: "Worm and parcel with the lay, turn and serve the other way."

Grindle was a wit. Rich shared with his daughter an exchange between Grindle and a tourist gazing at the sea:

> *Tourist: "Look at the codfish."*
> *Grindle: "Yeah, the only trouble is they've got hake skins on 'em."*

Grindle was working for Hinckley when he met Ruth Thurston, the daughter of Southwest Harbor's longtime postmaster, jeweler and juror. With her three sisters, Ruth attended the MacDuffie School for Girls and then the University of Maine. After a year, she met Ralph. She dropped out, and the couple married in 1935, beginning a marriage of seventy years.

Rich's disagreement with Hinckley, shortly after the end of the war, reportedly involved a twenty-eight-foot Carl Alberg–designed boat that had been built for Jim Willis, the owner of a local marine operation. Rich didn't like the boat's sheer, so when a second twenty-eight-footer was commissioned, he modified the design. Hutchins quoted Grindle's account of the incident: "Both boats were out on their moorings, side by side, and the second boat looked so much better that Jim was teed off. So Jim went to Henry and gave him hell. Henry cut the sheer down on Jim's Hinckley and Roger got sent to the spar shop."

Rich wasn't happy. He had been thinking about going into business for himself; the big barn next to his house would be perfect. The Grindle family lived across the street, so Rich went to Grindle and said, "Let's go build a boat in my barn," Grindle told Hutchins. (A third partner was Grindle's brother Steve, a sea captain living in Florida who provided additional financial backing.)

Fenton recalled the long, metal steambox hanging from the ceiling. "They would put the wood in there and leave it for hours. I think it still had the bark on the edges. When they pulled it out, it was so pliable they could bend it to the shape of the hull."

Unidentified Rich & Grindle boat outside the shop. *RuthAnn Fenton Collection.*

The partners' first boat, for the Frenchboro fisherman, hit the water in 1946. In 1948, they launched three boats: a power yacht for William Taylor, a Pulitzer Prize–winning sportswriter from Port Washington, New York; a thirty-two-foot fishing boat to summer resident Nelson Rockefeller; and the Maine Sea and Shore Fisheries Commission patrol boat, *Guardian*. Carroll Sargent Tyson Jr., the artist known for his bird paintings, commissioned a thirty-two-foot open boat with a streamlined windshield casing; the boat was later sold to a fisherman who, Rich told his daughter, "put a cabin on it and ruined the looks." Following that was a second open boat, twenty-five feet long, and a lobsterboat for a Southwest Harbor fisherman who was left-handed and asked for the boat to be rigged accordingly.

In December 1948, the partners signed a contract with Talbot Hamlin, a noted New York architect, preservationist and author. He and his wife, Jessica, enjoyed cruising on *Aquarelle*, their twenty-four-foot motor cruiser, along the East Coast. Long experience on *Aquarelle* helped them work out criteria for a second boat, according to their book, *We Took to Cruising*. It had to be seaworthy, strong and bigger, but not too big for easy handling. They preferred a trunk cabin, open cockpit with shelter, a small rig, ample locker space and a roomy cabin. Hamlin drew some sketches. As it happened, their nephew was Cyrus Hamlin, a naval architect whose designs included the well-known Hudson River sloop *Clearwater*. Cy had just opened an office in Southwest Harbor. He designed a thirty-one-foot power cruiser and recommended Rich & Grindle.

But Grindle fell ill and work was delayed. Sugar Fenton recalled an odd incident that occurred when she was a little girl. She had a doll cradle that needed to be repaired. "I took it across the street to Dad, and when he was hammering a nail in it, the hammer flew out of his hand," Fenton said. "He was weakened by a disease the doctors at first thought was polio. Within twenty-four to forty-eight hours, he was paralyzed."

Grindle was diagnosed with Guillain-Barre syndrome, a disease of the nervous system, and was unable to continue in boatbuilding. It's thought he might have contracted the disease during his time in Hawaii. He was laid up for a year, but through hard work, he regained his ability to walk. Rich built him a wheelchair to use while he was recuperating. "I remember him in our basement, working out with weights, with the sweat dripping off him," said Fenton. "He wound up with a limp, and he was able to manage his disease. He lived to be ninety. But it certainly changed things."

His wife, Ruth, went to work as head waitress for her sister, who owned the Dirigo Hotel on High Road. Another sister, from Massachusetts, helped care for the children in the summer. Ruth enjoyed her job. "She loved people," Fenton said. "And the guests learned she could make from scratch a cherry walnut angel cake, whipping by hand twelve egg whites. She made many cakes for them."

Grindle regained enough strength to open a convenience store on Main Street. Ruth made homemade ice cream to sell, using maple syrup and prepacked in flat-bottom cones. That was a huge seller. Grindle worked well into the evening, so the children visited him at the store. Grindle retired after thirty years but kept busy, visiting friends and even splicing rope again for Hinckley.

IN THE MEANTIME, THE Hamlins traveled to Southwest Harbor in July, thinking that their new cruiser would be ready for a midsummer cruise. "As Cy drove us to the hotel, we passed Rich & Grindle's shop—and there, looking out at us, was the graceful blue bow of Aquarelle II, her nose at the open doorway," the Hamlins wrote. "We stopped for a brief glimpse—and we were appalled."

The cabin top wasn't on, the ports hadn't been cut and the cockpit floor framing had only begun. Rich was unable to find more men to put on the job. Forced to wait, the Hamlins found themselves fascinated by the boatbuilding process. "We call Aquarelle II our 'hand-carved ship,'" they wrote. "All the moldings were planed out, not machine run. The builder himself shaped the stem head and the toe-rail breast hook with a favorite knife, and the beauty of the result shows the sensitive skill of the carver; his father formed and finished the grab rails as well as the spars. This handmade finish was slow, perhaps, but how we are going to enjoy the results in the years to come! The men loved their work; they had an affection for their tools and for the wood they were shaping; they were having fun; they were creating."

Launch day came in September, but it was delayed by a skunk. "To be launched, the boat had to be dragged out of the shop, into the busy road to Clark Point, and then back down a long gully to the ways; to do this dragging the one wrecking car of the town was needed. The night before, an expressman driving a load of fish had to turn out to avoid hitting a skunk (or what would have happened to the fish?) and tipped over and wrecked his truck. Of course the wrecking car's first job was to salvage the express truck, and that took all day!"

The following day was warm and sunny. *Aquarelle II* was loaded on a rugged launching cradle and pulled by "great jerks" down the hard road surface. "At the gutter she stopped. Much discussion. Then they commandeered another of the town's trucks—a heavy oil truck—and chained it to the wrecking car; both of these with a great pull snaked her over the gutter and up the crown of the road and switched her round to the required angle."

The boat reached the ways and slid into the water. A few days later, the Hamlins were happily away. Of Rich, they wrote that he "has the feel and the know-how, a deep love for boats, and a deep respect for the sea; he is also an excellent mechanic with a profound knowledge of gasoline engines and their ways. And he has an immaculate sense of standards."

RICH'S WIFE, LUCILE, RECEIVED beautiful bolts of fabric after her husband completed his next boat, a thirty-two-foot cabin cruiser, built like a lobsterboat but with a longer cabin, for John Wolf, a Fifth Avenue, New York textile manufacturer who had a summer home in Freeport. As Hutchins wrote:

> *In the spring of 1950, my mother and father delivered the boat to him on Long Island for what turned out to be a really special vacation. Mr. Wolf had someone show them around New York City and got them tickets to South Pacific.*
>
> *After they had returned home, a large box of fabric arrived, a gift from Mr. Wolf. Inside were bolts of material my mother had selected in New York, enough for living room curtains, plus a contrasting design that she*

John Wolf's boat, 1949. *Meredith Rich Hutchins Collection/SWHPLDA.*

used to reupholster the chairs and couch. A second box that Mr. Wolf had shipped to us consisted of fabric samples in many designs and colors. Supposedly these large squares were for Rich & Grindle to use as paint rags. Needless to say, my mother saw to it that they never went near the boat shop, and soon there were decorative pillows scattered about the house.

In the 1950s, after a few other boats, Rich returned to Hinckley to help build *Venturer*, the seventy-three-foot Sparkman & Stephens–designed yawl, the largest and penultimate wooden sailboat built by the yard.

Rich wasn't one to let one talent bog him down. He worked at a local car garage and served as a selectman in Tremont; he rowed across the harbor to the town hall to do payroll and hold office hours. "He was always for the underdog," said Hutchins. "There was a student at Tremont who went to high school, and there was a certain amount of culture shock, coming four miles. I remember they called him and said, 'We don't think this girl can hack it.' He persuaded them to give the girl more time. And she did graduate."

Mechanically inclined, he did his own automotive work and liked to take things apart. He flew a wood-and-fabric Piper Cub. Family lore has it that at different times, he gave a guy a ride for a bucket of smelts, which he sold to pay for gas; flew to Sorrento and landed on the ice in the harbor; flew lobsters to Boston in a seaplane; and flew under the Bucksport bridge. He was an outdoorsman and a Class B Maine Guide who spent a lot of time on Chesuncook Lake, an off-the-grid settlement in the North Woods, with his friend Francis "Mickey" Fahey. The two took a month-long trip to the remote Allagash River in the mid-1940s, and Rich made his own sleeping bag. "In my family, if they could make something, they never bought it," said Hutchins.

Fahey was himself an expert woodsman who had a passion for Maine's remote North Woods from a young age. In 1923, he was the state's youngest Maine Guide at age seventeen. Income derived from guided trips, trapping, cruising timber or working on the family farm dried up with the advent of the Depression. With a family to support (his daughter, Myrna, would become a well-known film and TV actor), he looked for new opportunities and landed a job in 1936 at Hinckley. During World War II, Fahey was yard superintendent, overseeing the company's feverish production for the military, according to "A Mentor Would Appear: Mick Fahey and the North Woods Way," a 1985 article by Jerry Stelmok published in *WoodenBoat* magazine.

After the war, Fahey served as an officer in the American Red Cross for ten years. Around 1955, he returned to the Hinckley yard, became general manager and oversaw production of the *Venturer* and the company's final wooden yacht, the forty-six-foot *Osprey*.

Fahey, like Rich, was always up for something new. In the winter of 1956–57, Bobby Rich subcontracted from his friend George Davis to build a seventeenth-century replica shallop, a small workboat. The thirty-three-foot replica would accompany a full-scale reproduction of the *Mayflower*, under construction in Devon, England, for display at the Massachusetts living history museum called Plimoth Plantation. The job called for craftsmen skilled in authentic wooden boat construction, using only hand tools. Bobby supplied the wood and sent Roger and Mickey to do the work.

The project prompted a to-do, making the front page of Plymouth's *Old Colony Memorial* newspaper. A photo shows Fahey in a fedora at a jaunty angle, his expression a bit Dean Martin. "The keel is plumb," he announces to onlookers.

Afterward, Rich was ready to quit building and go fishing. He didn't enjoy the business—"the losing-money part, that is," Hutchins said. He built a twenty-seven-foot lobsterboat and named it after his daughter; he later had his brother Ronald build a *Meredith II* and spent his days on the water. "He was one of these gentleman lobster fishermen. His boat was really a pleasure boat," recalled Chummy. "It was all fixed up down

Mick Fahey and Roger Rich caulk the Pilgrim shallop, 1956–57. *Meredith Rich Hutchins Collection/SWHPLDA. By permission of Plimouth Plantation.*

The lobsterboat *Meredith* at Castine. *Roger Rich photo/Meredith Rich Hutchins Collection/SWHPLDA.*

below. He was meticulous as hell. If you got a scratch on the side of the boat, he came and fixed it."

In the early 1960s, Roger decamped to Florida, following his old boss from Southwest Boat, Bink Sargent, who had become plant manager at Bertram Yacht in Miami. Later, Rich went to Mako Marine. Illness eventually prompted Rich and his second wife to move to Chicago, to be near his wife's daughter. He died in 1996 at eighty-two, having lived a life of many interests and a bit of mischief. "He could build anything," said Hutchins. "I don't think financially he was such a good businessman, certainly not like Bobby and Ronald. My father was a perfectionist and an artist, I will say that."

Chapter 4

RONALD RICH

FAMILY MAN AND HALL OF FAMER

I t's 1992, and Ronald Rich is reminiscing about his grandfather, "Talking John" Rich, who made boat models for his grandchildren. "I can remember my grandfather sitting on a doorstep," Ronald said in a Maine Maritime Museum/Filmex documentary, *Big Boats Made Small*. "He took a solid piece of wood, just the same as we did, and dug it out. But he never bothered to paint it. We had to put the waterline on and paint it. Then we tied a string on it, took a long stick and towed it parallel along the shore. Put a tin propeller on the bottom of it so it would make a noise."

An affable person, Ronald reckoned that his own drive to mess around with boats was ingrained by the habits of his forebears, making him—like his twin brother, Roger, and their younger brother, Bobby—part of a boatbuilding dynasty in Tremont and Southwest Harbor.

Rising early in the morning and working six days a week, he built boats for fishermen and yachters for more than half a century. Popular among lobster fishermen but preferring the finer work of pleasure boats, his designs were distinctive and his craftsmanship widely admired. He tried to retire in 1979, but the orders kept coming. Preferring to work alone, he produced about eighty boats in the thirty- to thirty-eight-foot range, at his peak averaging three per year. In 1996, he was inducted into the Maine Boatbuilders Hall of Fame.

Ronald was happy with his work. But above all, said his daughter, Judith deBray, he was a family man. His tendency toward solitude dissolved around his wife and their three daughters, his brothers and their families, his parents

Above: Roger, Ronald and Bobby, February 1917. *Judith deBray Collection.*

Left: Ronald Rich aboard *Marvel*, which he built in 1961. *Judith deBray Collection.*

and his wife's extended family. "Sunday was always picnic day," Judith said. "We were always active."

"Active" was practically Ronald's middle name while growing up. He was salutatorian of his class and kept busy with high school interests, helping to organize carnivals, May Day and theater productions, as well as playing baseball and basketball. "Ronald has no use for the girls whatever," his yearbook notes. "Ronald, you'd better watch out in the future because that beautiful curly hair has a great attraction for the girls."

For a guy with no use for girls, he won the lottery when he and his wife, Lizabeth Lawson—a nurse from Massachusetts whose family summered near his childhood home—had three daughters. Ronald both indulged and had high expectations of his girls. When not in school, they spent their childhoods roaming the neighborhood, playing baseball and kick the can and adventuring with their parents to islands and beaches and visits with the relatives. A thrill-seeker and a perfectionist who had a lot of friends but didn't crave much social life beyond his family, Ronald had a taste for the throttle wide open. In their twenties, he, Roger and others went in together to rent, and then buy, a small plane. Judith recalled her father's tales of dropping out of the sky to land at the last moment. The girls were drafted into his wild rides, careening through rough waves, salt spray flying, on the family boat *White Winger*, or deliberately spinning out his car on lake ice. The girls learned to water-ski behind *White Winger*—more like plowing through the water than skimming the surface. He loved to be outdoors.

"My father loved to go duck-hunting," said Judith. "He'd harvest cranberries every fall. I remember my parents coming back with bushel baskets of cranberries. He'd winnow them, and then my mother would can quarts and quarts of it. Out on Pond Island, we'd dig clams. He worked a lot, and he was strict, but what time he had, he spent with his family."

Ronald always regretted not going to college (and later required his daughters to go, making sure that he had the money to send them). Instead, he went straight from high school to build boats with his father, Cliff, and then to work for Chester Clement at Southwest Boat.

"He began working on a 60-footer they were building, smoothing up the bottom. He said that was the worst job a man could do," Jon Johansen wrote in 1996 for a Hall of Fame article. "Ronald worked for Clement for nearly three years and then moved across the harbor to work for Henry Hinckley. He worked on four or five yachts and then they began building boats for the war, mostly picket boats for the Army. He worked there all during the war, but after the war, things began to slow and he

White Winger. Judith deBray Collection.

was only there another year. Young men then were returning from the war and wanted a boat so as to go fishing."

Bobby, who had also been building war boats, was back at his own shop to accommodate this burgeoning demand. Ronald joined him, staying for nearly ten years. "He was a good worker," said Chummy. "Actually, he worked harder than any two fellas when he worked with Father. But he couldn't work shoulder to shoulder with anybody. You had to kind of put him on a job by himself. He'd go like hell."

In 1959, Ronald moved to his brother Roger's shop to build on his own. Johansen quoted him: "When I started out, I wasn't very confident. I went to Raymond Bunker and asked him if I could have one of his models to take the lines off of. He let me have it, but when I got it home and began to think about it, I said, 'If I am going to build boats, I better learn to design.' So I took the model back and designed my own boats. I didn't have any problems."

One of the boats, the *Meredith II*, was a thirty-five-footer for Roger. Roger worked on the boat, too, evenings and weekends. Occasionally, the brothers had their difference of opinions. For instance, there was the time Roger felt Ronald had compromised the oak framing that fastened the pilothouse to the hull. Fresh in Roger's mind was the March 1958 storm that resulted in the loss of two Cranberry Isles fishermen, whose bodies were found several days later aboard their vessel, grounded on the shore. Because the boat's pilothouse was separated from the hull, people speculated that the men died of exposure. Roger, both a lobster fisherman and a boatbuilder, didn't want that to happen on his boat. He wanted the four oak posts to go down through the trunk. Ronald had cut into them to accommodate window hardware. "They had a hell of an argument," Meredith said.

Roger kept the boat for three years and then sold it to Sheldon "Snicker" Damon, a guy with a sense of humor who named it *Mum's Mink* and used it twenty years for fishing, chartering and family picnics. It became a familiar fixture off Northeast Harbor and was later restored by Snicker's sons.

When Roger moved to Florida in the early 1960s, Ronald built his own shop, working alone except to have Chummy in to do mechanical and electrical work. He was eager to be helpful, Chummy remembered. "When you went over there, he waited on you hand and foot, to the point where he was underfoot. If he'd just gone about and done his thing, left me to myself—I knew where all the tools were, I didn't really need him. But he thought he had to wait on ya every minute to make sure you didn't need anything."

Ronald's courtesy and lack of guile won over a prospective customer, A.A. Loomis, of Marshfield, Massachusetts. Writing in a letter to the editor in *Maine Coast Fisherman* in 1964, Loomis said that he was attracted to the "handsome rugged-looking" Ronald Rich boats seen on the Massachusetts shore. One of the owners was "an enthusiastic booster for Ronald Rich as a boatbuilder and a fine gentleman." With his wife, Loomis, who appreciated Ronald's zero-pressure sales approach, signed a contract for a thirty-four-foot pleasure craft and visited periodically to check on progress.

"We found Ronald to be not only an exceptionally fine boatbuilder, but also to be most cooperative in translating our thoughts and wishes on cabin and cockpit layout and details into being," Loomis wrote. "The second weekend in May, in the face of small craft warnings (which proved to be an understatement), we brought the new boat down to Marshfield in two

Above: A new cruiser at Ronald's shop, 1964. *W.H. Ballard photo/SWHPLDA.*

Left: Ronald Rich with a half-model he made. *Judith deBray Collection.*

daytime hops. We faced high winds, rough terrain, and fog, but the boat came through it all like a champion. The boat proved that a craft built by Ronald Rich can take it; in fact, the boat can take a lot more than the people in it can."

AS THE GIRLS GREW into their teen years, Ronald found a new companion in a little wire-haired fox terrier named Laddy. The girls had always wanted a dog, of course. But Laddy, who was hit by a truck, and his three successors, each named Ruff, became a fixture in Ronald's arms, especially after Lizabeth died in 1978. Lizabeth's death hit hard, and the girls were grown and gone. Ronald built himself a boat to keep busy, but he was never happy with it. Without his family, it wasn't the same.

Two years later, at age seventy-one, he launched his last boat. "I was beginning to get tired," he said in the documentary. Ruefully, he said that he approached retirement with the idea of capturing something of his wife. "I thought, 'My wife used to have roses,' and I thought I'd plant some roses and have a little garden. But that wasn't it. I didn't like to do it."

Always one to make wooden furnishings for the house and boat models for the kids, he began making lobster weathervanes, giving them to friends and neighbors. He walked, connected with neighbors, sat down by the town dock and, always a welcome presence, visited the various boat shops in town to see what was going on. He couldn't help but notice how much more nimbly and quickly he was able to plank up a boat compared to his younger colleagues—back in the day, when he had the strength.

"I miss it now," he said, twelve years after Lizabeth's passing and five years before his own. "I'd like to be able to start over."

Chapter 5
BUNKER AND ELLIS

HOW TWO MEN PLAYED POOL AND
BECAME BOATBUILDING ICONS

W e worked nights, Thanksgiving, New Year's, even Christmas," Raymond Bunker said in 1979, not long after his thirty-two-year partnership with Ralph Ellis ended. "Often, we worked until nine o'clock or midnight, just the two of us, and we sometimes built four boats in a winter."

Before Bunker and Ellis teamed up in 1946 to build boats, both had developed reputations around the waterfront as hardworking and knowledgeable. Ellis was a fisherman who helped run a commercial wharf. Bunker was the head foreman of a large boatyard and ran private yachts during the summer. Bunker wanted to build a boat for himself and had plenty of experience with design. Ellis had a workshop on his property and wanted to learn more about woodworking. They got together evenings just to pass the time on this new endeavor, so they called the first boat they built *Evening Pastime*. A neighboring fisherman liked the looks of *Evening Pastime*. He asked them to build him a new lobsterboat. Bunker and Ellis liked to work hard and didn't mind putting in the extra hours, so they took on the job.

They thought they'd build mainly for fishermen. But things evolved after Bunker built for his own use another boat, *Sueann*, in 1949. Thanks to his summer work hiring out himself and his boat for the use of Northeast Harbor residents, *Sueann* caught the eye of a wealthy summer resident, who wanted to charter it. Bunker persuaded the resident instead to have him design and build a yacht. This was a seminal moment for what would eventually become the highly regarded and iconic lobsteryacht, a combination of gorgeous topside and rich interior wedded to the stable and sturdy lobsterboat hull.

Waterbed, formerly *Arethusa III*, built in 1967—at forty-four feet the partners' largest boat. *W.H. Ballard Photo/Bunker Family Collection.*

More yachters came, intrigued by the aesthetics, performance and comfortable feeling of these boats. Most of the Bunker and Ellis repertoire is still turning heads, with beautiful lines and custom finish work in teak and mahogany like rare gems in an industry of mass production.

Over three decades, the partners turned out fifty-nine wooden powerboats. They built in the winter, starting in October or November, shutting the shop down when spring rolled around to fish and run yachts. "They said it was too hot to build a boat in there anyway," recalled Ralph's son Don who, with his older brother, Dennis, took over the shop after they retired and began building customized fiberglass boats.

The shop was usually quiet—no radio, just the sound of hand tools. Bunker always had a pipe clenched between his teeth; it wriggled a bit when he got excited. Although the shop could be hot enough to drive Ellis to take out the windows and wear bathing trunks, Bunker wore long underwear, shirt and pants, a pullover sweater and overalls. "One day," recalled Don, "Father came in for supper, and he said, 'Well, it must have got hot today—Raymond took off his sweater!'"

Bunker at the shop, 1978. *Bunker Family Collection.*

The two men understood each other. "They very seldom spoke," said Don. "If they were under the boat planking, they didn't have to say, 'Pick your end up. Put your end down.' If Dad was holding the end of the plank and Raymond was starting it, Dad could almost tell by the feel, when he'd slide the plank up, which way Raymond wanted it to go."

Although Ellis didn't know the trade, at the start, his innate knowledge of the sea was an invaluable asset. "Because he was a fisherman, he knew what a boat had to do in all kinds of sea conditions," said Dennis. "One of the unique things about design that my father always told me was that you want a boat that's good in a following sea. Because if she's not, the sea will lift her stern and put her bow in 'up to her chocks!' he'd say. Also, you don't want her too deep forward, or it makes a rudder on the bow."

BUNKER WAS BORN IN 1906 and grew up on Great Cranberry Island, one of six children and the son of a fisherman. The family's roots went back to the mid-1700s with the arrival of one of the first European settlers on the island.

Rugged and smart, Bunker was popular and known as a kidder. As a teenager, he tried going to the mainland for high school, in northern Maine, where his older sister lived. "He didn't last a year," said his daughter,

Susan Bunker Newman. "Hated living away from the ocean. So his formal education ended, and he went back to the island."

Bunker got his father's small boat, powered by a ten-horse, make-or-break Bridgeport, and began transporting his uncle to Southwest Harbor for his job at the boatyard of Chester Clement, an influential builder. Clement ended up giving young Bunker a job sweeping floors and keeping the shop clean for two dollars a day. After a week, Bunker got to do two or three little jobs working on boats.

Interviewed in 1974 for the GHMM collection, Bunker remembered his encounters with Clement: "He says, 'Hell, you are just as good as any other fella. I'll get you some tools, I know what you need. Monday morning you go to work same wages they're getting, five dollars a day.' That made me feel pretty good."

Bunker worked for Clement for ten years, commuting from Great Cranberry, until Clement's untimely death from an automobile accident in 1937. Lennox "Bink" Sargent and Henry Hinckley bought Clement's shop, changed the name to Southwest Boat and appointed Bunker head foreman in time to supervise more than one hundred employees building mine yawls for the navy during World War II. After the war, Bunker received a navy

Bunker builds a cruiser, *Patsy S.*, at the Hinckley shop, 1938. *W.H. Ballard Photo/Bunker Family Collection.*

citation and stayed on to design and supervise construction of commercial fishing boats, up to one hundred feet long.

During summers, he hired out as a private yacht captain for wealthy residents in Northeast Harbor. A well-known presence at Clifton Dock, he was admired for his professionalism and knowledge. At the same time, on Great Cranberry, Bunker met a farm girl from northern Maine. Gail Patterson was on the island by chance. She planned to work at L.L. Bean for the summer but got a bad case of tonsillitis. When she recuperated, she joined her older sister, who was working at the island's fancy Hamor's Tea House. "They met in the summer and were married in October," Susan said. "Dad was a sought-after bachelor, I gather."

Gail didn't care for island life. It was confining, especially in the winter, when it was difficult to get off. The couple moved to Southwest Harbor, buying the house they would own for some fifty years. Nearby was Jim's Place, a soda fountain and pool hall. Bunker loved to play pool and was good at it. He was there one evening when he got talking with Ralph Ellis, a hardworking fisherman and a family man.

Ellis later described the interaction: "Raymond made the statement, 'If I had a place to build a boat, I would be doing so instead of wasting my time

Hushai II, built in 1956, seen here in 1987. *Bunker/Newman Family Collection.*

playing pool.'" Ellis quoted himself: "I have a shop but I know very little about building a boat. However, if you wish, I'll put my shop up against your 'know-how.' The following morning Raymond ordered lumber for two 34s."

ELLIS WAS BORN IN 1910 on the southwest coast of Nova Scotia, in a fishing village near Digby. His grandfather Charles Dennis Ellis was a Canadian boatbuilder and sea captain of a schooner from Massachusetts. His father, Ralph Sr., was a fisherman. During the Depression, the family moved to Brockton, Massachusetts. Ralph Sr. didn't like the city and moved to Mount Desert Island to resume fishing.

When Ralph Jr. was fourteen or fifteen, his mother died. His father met another woman on Great Cranberry. In those days, a teenager was expected to fill a man's shoes, so Ralph Jr. took care of his two young sisters, Dorothy (called Dot) and Hilda, who were perhaps eleven and thirteen and thought the world of their older brother. They lived in a one-room house on the Manset shore. (They also had an older sister, Margaret, married to Malcolm Ward.)

Young Ralph dropped out of high school to work. It was a rough existence. Ralph sawed wood, cut ice in the winter to go to the big J.L. Stanley freezer nearby and baited trawl for fifty cents a tub to make enough money to buy a few things—milk and potatoes—to keep the family going.

Back in the day, people took care of one another. Folks paid Ralph for his work but also gave him a little extra—maybe eggs or milk. Ralph made biscuits for himself and his sisters, getting a cookfire going from green alders, whose sap produced a hot flame. He earned a reputation as a hard worker. In the 1920s, he started working for a fisherman named Harvard Beal. The young men fished through the winter, going to Mount Desert Rock, a windswept island twenty-five miles offshore, landing the catch in Beal's twenty-eight-foot boat. Once, Beal was at the helm when Ellis spotted a freighter coming at them. Ellis raced back to grab the wheel and spun them out of the way—almost rolling the boat—just in time.

During summers, Ellis sailed for two prosperous Northeast Harbor summer families. One was the McCabes. He would take Thomas McCabe out on Somes Sound. "They'd buy some lobsters and put down their anchor," Dennis said. "Then they'd cook and eat those lobsters together. There they were, a fisherman and the president of this great, big Scott Paper Company, and they got along just fine."

Harvard had a sister, Velora. Their father was Vinal Beal, a lighthouse keeper at Mount Desert Rock. Velora was eight when her mother moved

Ralph Ellis caulks *Irona*. *Ellis Family Collection.*

the children to the mainland for school. The family lived in a house near Ralph's; Velora sometimes played with his little sisters. Her mother thought the world of Ralph. "Every time he went fishing, which was every day with my brother," Velora said in a GHMM interview, "we could see from my mother's house where Ralph put the porch light on when he got in from fishing. So I'd go to the door, when he took his buckets down to get some water out of the well, we'd holler over to him, 'Ralphie, Mama's got your supper ready here for you!' We took awful good care of him and Dorothy and Hilda."

Velora grew up and attracted Ralph's eye. They married in 1935 and bought a small house in Manset. There was a small workshop on the adjacent property, so Ralph bought that, too, for $500.

Ralph worked hard to make sure his family never worried about where the next potato or egg was coming from. Dennis remembered his father's fishing days well: "He loved to work; he loved everything he did. I remember he was always whistling or singing. As a boy, I might wake up at one or two in the morning, and he'd be out in the kitchen. Now, what is he doing up at this time? Well, he'd be going out fishing, out to the islands to set tubs of trawl with Uncle Harvard. And he wouldn't get back in until—well, he used to eat supper on the boat."

Even though he worked most of the time, he loved doing little things for his family. One night for supper, he promised Velora a treat. He'd make her something great that she'd never eaten before. So he concocted pancakes with chicken in them. "He was great at making pancakes because that's all he had when he was a kid," she said.

They were wonderful parents—and frugal. Even though they could afford to buy lobster, Dennis recalled his mother picking up lobster bodies from a nearby restaurant and extracting every molecule of meat for the family's meal. She was also charitable. "She said she felt it was an obligation to help out if she possibly could. She would give to the end."

It was years before the family got a car, and when they did, it was barely used. "I remember when I got my driver's license," said Don. "I said, 'Well, can I take the car and go uptown?' ["Uptown" meant Southwest Harbor, a mile away.] And he looked at me like I was nuts. 'Well, what are you going to do uptown?' I said, 'I just want to take a ride uptown.' 'No, why would you want to do that? It'd just waste gas.' They thought a trip uptown was a big trip."

Raymond enjoyed Ralph's company. Velora recalled Raymond saying, "If anyone can't get along with Ralph Ellis, there's something wrong with them."

They earned probably two dollars per hour and never put down their hammer or screwdriver until the job was done, even if it took them until midnight to finish it, she said. Ralph liked the customers, but mostly he let Raymond do the talking. Ralph had a reputation for being soft-spoken. "Soft-spoken?!" Don exclaimed, then joked, "I didn't think he could talk until I was about fifteen years old. Never said two words, never complained about anything."

But Ralph had a sense of humor. Don remembered that he built a doghouse for their childhood beagle, Snookie. "This was the Taj Mahal of doghouses," he said. One night, Don got home and found there was a light on in the doghouse. "So I said, 'Dad, what's the light in the doghouse for?' He said, 'Well, she likes to read at night.'"

THE BUNKER AND ELLIS shop was an unimpressive building. As the age of fiberglass rumbled in, Raymond put up a plaque: "If God wanted fiberglass boats, he would have planted fiberglass trees." Inside, it hardly seemed the builders could stand back far enough to see how the lines of a new hull were shaping up.

Dennis recalled his father and Bunker began lofting around August. Bunker carved the half-models (later, Ellis also designed boats). Ellis painted the floor white and marked a grid with six-inch spacing. Together, they lifted the lines from the model and transferred them to scale. "One time, I remember, they drafted a hull and the only piece of paper Raymond could find was building paper, and the thickness of the pencil was probably two inches," Dennis recalled. "But the boats always came out perfect."

Fairlee (later *Bagpiper*), built in 1955, with young Don Ellis in the background. *W.H. Ballard photo/Bunker Family Collection.*

Kittiwake II, built in 1964. *Bunker/Newman Family Collection.*

Rambler, built in 1967. *Bunker Family Collection.*

New boats were dragged on a cradle out the front doors and down the hill to the shore, where they were "rocked down" with beach rocks. The rising tide floated them free. "They'd turn the key, the engine would go and they'd take off. Everything worked," Dennis said. "That's the way it was."

Boats were narrower in those days, not having to carry big engines or the mass of traps customary today. With a semi-displacement, built-down hull, the Bunker and Ellis style was known for the "rightness" of its proportions, the sweep of the sheer and the sweet curves of the tumblehome. Each boat was a custom work of art. Varnished mahogany cabinsides, shelters and coamings sparkled in the sun, catching the eye. Open cockpits and cabins were spacious and inviting. The boats were a distinctive breed.

Around the waterfront, the boats were effective advertising; often, new orders came in at the dock, with nothing more than a verbal okay. Launching three or four new vessels a year during the 1950s, the partners produced a string of pleasure boats for the area's wealthy summer residents. One of them, today named *Adequate*, is in the hands of an inveterate Bunker and Ellis enthusiast who never thought he'd buy a powerboat.

A sunny person who likes to say "oh golly" and "God bless you," Rod Lucas splits his year between Southwest Harbor and Connecticut. He knew Bunker from a distance when he was a child, and he'd always admired the duo's boats. "When you see somebody like that, you kind of hold them up and deify them because, as far as powerboats, I thought there was nothing to equal them in beauty," he said. "I still feel that way."

One day, in 1970, Lucas noticed that a twenty-year-old Bunker and Ellis was on the market. "I got very excited because if I had ever wanted a powerboat, that was my dream boat—to have a boat that was built by Bunker and Ellis," Lucas recalled.

The price was just $4,000—the temptation irresistible. A gem that evoked the partners' early career, the boat was built for a wealthy summer resident in 1950, just four years after they started production. Lucas called the broker. There was a waiting list. He was number twelve. He bided his time as a succession of number ones backed out. "I got nervous. I said, 'Something must be wrong with her.'"

When he reached number three, he called Bunker and asked him to survey the hull. "He said, 'That old piece of junk?! Hell, that thing will probably sink before I can look at it,'" Lucas recalled. Bunker replaced some fastenings and a punky plank, but otherwise the boat was sound.

Lucas reached number one. He sent his check and traveled with a friend from Connecticut to Southwest Harbor. He encountered a "short gentleman" at the dock. "He said, 'What are you looking for?' I said, 'I'm not looking for anything. I got that Bunker and Ellis down there on the dock. I just bought her!' I was really excited about having it. He said, 'God, you bought that boat?' And I said, 'Yes, sir, I did!' And he said, 'She won't make it out of the harbor!'"

Lucas went to shop for provisions for the cruise back to Connecticut. At the grocery, he got to bragging about his new boat. "That short gentleman was in there, and they were all laughing." It was Ralph Ellis. "He thought that was a riot because I got a little nervous about what he told me. A wonderful friendship grew over the years."

Lucas "cheated" and stole the name of his parents' launch, *Adequate*, for his boat. The little launch was "barely adequate" for his mother's picnic parties. The Bunker and Ellis? More than adequate. "It is the most beautiful hull going through the water. It just is the most easy-running hull. I do love her," he said.

Apparently, one of the area's high-end yacht builders agreed. Around 1990, Lucas got a call from the Hinckley Company, interested in taking a ride on the old boat and measuring its lines. "When they decided, apparently, to build what is now called the Picnic Boat, they picked the *Adequate* as being what they envisioned conceptually, in the early stages," Lucas noted.

BY 1965, BUNKER AND Ellis had slowed down, launching mostly one boat per year. In the 1970s, the duo began building wide-bodied lobsterboats, some later transformed by other builders into lobsteryachts. Their last boat was *Sister's Pride*, launched in 1978. Rigged for scallop fishing, it sank several years later, possibly holed by one of the steel doors on the drag. (The crew was picked up by another fishing boat.)

With the completion of *Sister's Pride*, Bunker was ready to retire—Ellis, not so much. The latter was a force to be reckoned with and not at all averse to fiberglass. Ellis designed one thirty-four-foot and one thirty-eight-foot lobsteryacht for fiberglass production at the nearby yard of his good friend Lee S. Wilbur. He and Dennis designed a nineteen-foot wooden boat to go punt-fishing and, at the behest of a friend, lengthened the hull to make a twenty-foot plug for fiberglass production. This occurred at the former Bunker and Ellis shop, which operated under the name of R. Dennis Ellis. Father and son designed a twenty-eight-footer, and Wilbur came into the project to make the top mold; with that, they formed the Ellis Boat Company.

When Don also expressed an interest in boatbuilding, Ralph urged Dennis to take him on. Wilbur sold his share to Don and continued the work at his

The lobsterboat *Elizabeth Battles. Bunker/Newman Family Collection.*

own shop. Dennis would eventually leave Ellis Boat to continue his career as a pharmacist. "My brother has done an excellent job of maintaining the Ellis name," Dennis said.

Ralph stayed on with Don until his death in 1994 at age eighty-three. Bunker had died just two months previously, at age eighty-seven. "My father was out in the shop two weeks before he died," Don recalled. "I think he knew it was the last time. He told my mother to call me and tell me he was coming out. He made sure everyone knew he was out there, looking around."

Chapter 6
JARVIS NEWMAN
EARLY FIBERGLASS TRENDSETTER

W e'd be having dinner or dessert out on the porch on a Sunday night, in the summer, and these people, sometimes the old-timers, would drive up and they wouldn't even get out of their car; they'd converse from the porch, they'd just pull in and they'd talk. And he sold boats that way."

Recently, at the brokerage firm that Jarvis Newman started when he retired from boatbuilding in 1978, the noise of grinding and hammering can be heard from the cavernous shop out back as a few Friendship sloop owners get their boats ready for the summer. Newman's daughter, Kathe Walton, described her father's astounding success, in the 1970s, as a leader in advancing the use of fiberglass for powerboat and sailboat construction. In his heyday, boats popped out of his Southwest Harbor shop at the rate of one every two weeks. "Why don't you build me one of those 36s?…Same when Dad would mow the lawn. These guys would just swing by and just roll out whatever they probably got from the catch of the day, and they'd give you a thousand dollars as a down payment and a handshake. That was it."

The Newman family is immersed in the local boatbuilding scene and rooted in the locale going back to the eighteenth century. A fellow named Samuel Hadlock arrived on the Cranberry Isles and came to an ignominious end in 1790 when he was hanged for murder. Hadlock's son and grandson were also named Samuel. The son led the hard life of an offshore fisherman before settling down. The grandson was a visionary. Born in 1792, he left the Cranberries to take up sealing and whaling in the far north and then took

The Newman 36 *Patriot*, 2007. *Jarvis Newman Collection.*

two native people and an exhibit of native items on tour through Europe. He married a Prussian woman, Dorothea Albertina Wilhelmina Celeste Hadlock, and returned with her to Great Cranberry Island. Their story is written up in the 1934 book *God's Pocket* by Rachel Field.

Newman's grandfather Lyle is a descendant of the Cranberry-settling Hadlocks and was also a man of the sea. A Southwest Harbor lobster dealer and fisherman, Lyle had two sixty- to eighty-foot lobster smacks. He'd go to Nova Scotia, buy lobsters, bring them back and sell them to a Boston dealer. He was on the water until his late eighties; he died at age ninety-eight.

Lyle taught his son Laurence to fish. As a kid, Laurence had his own boat. Then he tried life at a Boston prep school and MIT, where he studied electrical engineering. Laurence married a smart go-getter, Eleanor Jarvis, and went to work for the Southern New England Telephone Company in Connecticut. But corporate life didn't suit him. When he learned that he had diabetes (in the 1940s a treatable disease, but still dire), Laurence decided to live "what 'little' life he had left the way he wanted," as his obituary notes. That meant being on the sea, at home by the waterfront where he grew up.

At age forty, Laurence returned to his roots in Southwest Harbor, with Eleanor and their three children in tow, and joined his father to form a lobster-buying and fishing business. He had a thirty-two-foot boat built at Southwest

Boat, but it didn't work out because the engine was too far forward and the boat was unbalanced. The Rich brothers in nearby Richtown built him a thirty-foot boat with a ten-foot beam. It was "a good, fat ride"—dangerously wide, according to Laurence and Eleanor's son, Jarvis, in a 1999 interview for the GHMM collection. Jarvis was a kid of thirteen or fourteen when he and his father were heading out to fish off Mount Desert Rock and the sea picked up the boat and almost rolled it over.

Jarvis recalled baiting bags for his father after school. Come summer, he went along with his father, from 2:00 a.m. to 5:00 p.m. the next evening, staying out all night, mostly at Mount Desert Rock and mostly tub-trawling for hake, halibut and codfish. One time they got a large tuna on a harpoon. From August through November, Laurence set two hundred lobster traps, "a tremendous number" for the time. "He made a very good living on that," Jarvis said. "Sometimes when the fishing was good, he'd get a pound per trap." At the time, lobster sold for about thirty cents per pound.

Laurence had a close call one night, coming in from Mount Desert Rock in thick fog with a load of pollock. He was cleaning fish at the stern with the tiller in rudder position when the fog lifted just enough to reveal Bunker's Ledge, dead ahead, maybe fifty yards distant. He lunged forward, grabbed the wheel and spun it. By a stroke of good fortune, a large roller carried his boat past the ledge.

Laurence expected to die young because of his illness, but he lived to age ninety-six.

SQUARE-JAWED AND TRIM, with a purposeful look in his eyes, Jarvis as a young man left his childhood home in Southwest Harbor to get an associate's degree in aircraft maintenance, spend time in the army and worked for General Electric Aviation in Cincinnati, Ohio, where he worked with the test program that designed and built jet engines. He was there for three years, testing big J47 turbojets for fighter planes in the Korean War. But Newman didn't like the area. "It was hot and dry, and I missed being on the ocean," he said. So he finagled a transfer to GE in Lynn, Massachusetts, where he tested helicopter engines and wrote technical publications.

Newman came home one summer vacation to visit his family. One day, he stopped by his aunt's apartment, which overlooked Main Street opposite the movie theater. He noticed a young woman emerging from the theater. Susan Bunker was one of Raymond and Gail Bunker's four children. The Bunker family lived in town, and Susan had taken her younger brothers to the show. She was sixteen.

Susan recounted, "He said to his aunt, 'Who is that?' And she told him. So he zipped down the stairs and sort of walked up as far as St. John's church, and he said, 'Where are you going to college this fall?' I said, 'I'll be a junior in high school.' He sort of made a U-turn." Several years later, when he moved to Lynn, he learned that Susan was in Boston at the Katharine Gibbs School. He called. "We started dating in January. We married at the end of October," Susan said.

Susan went to work for the Sylvania Electric Company in Salem. In Lynn, Jarvis decided that he probably wasn't going to go any higher at GE. The couple moved to Nashua, New Hampshire, where Jarvis worked for the Stanley Elevator Company, founded by a man who grew up in Bass Harbor. "They needed somebody in the state of Maine to install and service elevators," said Jarvis. "Stanley elevators are very different. They're not cable. They're hydraulic with a pump. It was the latest thing on an elevator."

After a while, the couple moved back to Southwest Harbor with their two small children to be near family. That summer, they were at a party and ran into Bob Hinckley, the eldest son of Henry Hinckley, founder of the Henry R. Hinckley Company. Bob needed someone in the fiberglass department. Newman worked there for the next few years. "Bob and I grew up together," said Newman. "I ran the glass department—as though I knew anything about glass. We built one boat a week."

It was the mid-1960s; fiberglass was a growing market. Hinckley was producing Bermuda 40s and Pilots. Newman earned $1.95 an hour. "It was fun," he recalled. "And women were very good fiberglassers because they have the patience—they see more than men do. The hull—piece of cake, anybody could do that. That's just straight going. But the deck, all the corners and crevices, you've got to make sure you get all the air out of the glass."

He got an idea to try a fiberglass project on his own. He pulled a mold from an eleven-foot skiff and produced a fiberglass version. He set one on display at his grandparents' house in Manset, asking $375. "His father and grandfather laughed at him, saying no one would pay that kind of money for a newfangled fiberglass boat," Walton said. His first customer bought two, and Newman sold a couple of dozen all together. Still, he wasn't entirely happy with the boat. That's when his father-in-law, Raymond Bunker, offered key advice: "If you're going to build a boat, build a good one."

Bunker offered a handsome twelve-foot skiff designed and built by his uncle, Arthur Spurling, to use as a plug. Newman took a mold off the tender and built a fiberglass version, although not an exact replica. Newman gave it a wineglass stern, took an inch off the sheer, added cove stripes,

Jarvis Newman, in the late 1960s, rows an early twelve-foot tender. *Jarvis Newman Collection.*

changed the keel a little and cut the stern down two inches. He estimated that the fiberglass version weighed one hundred pounds less than its wooden predecessor. More than five hundred twelve-footers would be built over the years. "It really took off," Newman noted. "The eleven-footer did all right, but nothing like the twelve-footer."

Next, Newman had his eye on the wooden Friendship sloops seen in many Maine harbors. He was particularly taken by a sloop named *Old Baldy*, built a few years earlier by James Rockefeller Jr. in Camden. Newman got permission from the owner to pull a mold and built the first fiberglass Friendship.

Given his success, Newman realized that there might be an untapped market for fiberglass workboats that could be quickly produced to a uniform standard. He recalled meeting Frank Cram, who owned an elegant thirty-six-foot Bunker and Ellis yacht named *Irona*. He convinced Cram to let him pull a mold. "I said, 'Look, if I take your boat for the winter, I'll bring it back to you in the spring and I'll pay for the storage. And I'll completely take all the paint off the hull and repaint it for nothing,'" recalled Newman. "It was a very big win-win for him. It was a scary thought, taking a mold off a boat like that, because if it ever stuck—oooh, that would be a disaster."

But the idea worked. Since its debut in 1971, Newman produced eighty-nine for both pleasure and commercial buyers. "Dad really jumped off the

The Pemaquid 25 *Resolute. Jarvis Newman Collection.*

map with that," Walton said. That same year, Newman bought a Friendship sloop for himself, a thirty-one-footer named *Dictator*, badly in need of repair. Newman filled *Dictator* with Styrofoam so he could float it to his shop from Stonington. His wooden boatbuilding neighbor Ralph Stanley helped rebuild it, and Newman began to produce fiberglass sailboats. Both the "Dictator" model and the twenty-five, the "Pemaquid" model, have been popular among Friendship sloop enthusiasts, who bought nearly forty over the next decade.

Another hot item was the forty-six-foot design he commissioned in the 1970s, a roomy craft that attracted the attention of performing artist Billy Joel; ninety were produced. The first forty-six was snapped up by Curtis Blake, co-founder of Friendly's Ice Cream, who had a summer home in Northeast Harbor. (Blake's boat was destroyed several years ago in a storm in the Galapagos Islands. Newman keeps a chunk of the keel in his office as a memento.) "He wanted a twenty-foot living room. And if he wants it, I think he can have it," Newman said of Blake's specifications. "And he would give us ice cream." "He brought boxloads of Harbor Bars," Walton fondly remembered of the ice cream sandwiches that Blake's daughter produced in Trenton.

Newman did the interiors on the first few boats but was soon farming out the finish work. Through the 1970s, Newman's boats, basically, gave other

A Newman 46 workboat. *Jarvis Newman Collection.*

The Newman 46 *Frolic*. *Jarvis Newman Collection.*

shops a start. "Lee Wilbur sprang up. Tom Morris took the Friendships," said Walton, citing prominent local builders. "Mac Pettegrow. They did the finish work for primarily Newman hulls. They've branched out, and they do different things now. But back then, Dad supplied the hulls, and those men finished them off."

But Newman installed the engines himself. "The hull was done with the engine, drive train, transmission and propeller shaft because I didn't want someone else putting an engine in crooked and saying, 'Oh, that Newman, that's a terrible boat,'" he said. "I didn't want vibration. They could say, if it shook, 'Oh, that's a damn Newman boat. That's no good.' So I made sure the engines were put in. It's so easy to do it right. You just lower it and glass it. It's perfect and simple."

In 1978, the business was sold to Lewis Moore of Northeast Harbor, and currently, CW Hood Yachts in Marblehead, Massachusetts, owns the powerboat molds. Newman retains his Friendship sloop molds, and Newman & Gray, on Great Cranberry Island, owns the molds for Newman's tender. "I just wanted to do something different that was modern and easy," Newman recalled.

"That's the beginning of the industry," added Walton. She turned to her dad. "I would say you were very much progressive. You had a vision where it was going."

Chapter 7
STEVE SPURLING

WHO ARE YOU!?

On a visit to Jarvis Newman's shop, his daughter, Kathe Walton, gave me the lowdown on framed photos of old yachts hanging on the walls. Among them is a picture of *Maddy Sue*, previously *Trail Away*, built by Chester Clement for Captain Francis Spurling. Walton mentioned that Captain Francis's son, Steve, lives with his wife, Arlene, two doors down from the Newman shop. I've probably noticed the Whitehalls on the lawn. Hard to believe he's ninety-something and still building boats. And Arlene is a seamstress, selling her wares at various co-ops. "They stay so busy," she said. "They're both remarkable."

Newman, who is semi-retired, strolled in from the back office. "He needs to do something, just like I do," he said. "I'm not sitting home watching TV. Got to keep going."

Walton caught sight of someone coming through the back workshop. "Oh, oh, here's trouble," she joked. I turned and saw an older man with a friendly face and a roguish gleam in his eye. It's Spurling, who swings by Newman's shop regularly to chat. He homed in on me, cheerfully demanding, "Who are you?!" He turned to Newman and Walton for the latest gossip on the neighborhood's rental houses, which apparently could use better upkeep. Taking advantage of a break, I asked Spurling if I could visit his shop.

He's hard of hearing. "You coming now? Is that what she said?" he asked Walton.

"You've got to yell," Walton told me.

"Okay, dear," he said, sliding into a chuckle. "C'mon. What do you want, take you by the hand?"

We headed outside, Spurling forging ahead. "C'mon on!" he urged, walking half a block and crossing his yard to a shop out back. Inside was the usual workshop clutter: piles of sawdust; coffee cans full of fastenings; stray drill bits, clamps and rolls of tape; lead weights, sandpaper rounds, measuring tapes, hand tools, shop lamps, lumber and boat hardware lined up around a snub-nosed pram under construction. His design is based on a small Norwegian boat once used for light fishing. Out back, he opened up some storage shelters and revealed half a dozen small boats—finely wrought craft, brightwork gleaming in the sun, built from cedar on oak, with mahogany and oak trim.

We headed over to the house, and I met Arlene, hospitable, friendly and notably fit in her late eighties, thanks to regular exercise. These days, Spurling continued, small boats keep him busy enough. After all, he's been at it nearly eighty years. In the early days, growing up on Great Cranberry Island, he rode Raymond Bunker's boat every morning to Southwest Harbor, and back in the late afternoon, so he could work for the Southwest Boat Corporation; the crew was building a ninety-foot wooden dragger outdoors, enduring all kinds of weather.

Life took a turn when World War II stormed in, and it's not something he likes to discuss. But Arlene wants people to know, and she showed me his citation, which notes that Spurling joined the heavy machine gun section in Company D of the Army's 351st Infantry Regiment. His section, supporting the assault on Sarti, Italy, came under intense enemy fire, killing the platoon leader and six other members of the company. Spurling assumed command, reorganized the men and kept them alert and supplied with ammunition. He was awarded a Bronze Star for heroic achievement in action. "Sergeant Spurling's brave and fearless actions under fire reflect great credit upon himself and exemplify the high traditions of the United States Army," the citation reads.

Spurling returned home to work a while longer at Southwest Boat. But mainly, for the next fifty years, he oversaw the fleet of boats belonging to a wealthy Northeast Harbor summer family. During the winter, he worked for area boatbuilders, including the John M. Williams Company and Ralph Stanley, who is Spurling's cousin. Spurling maintained a long relationship with the Williams yard, where he produced fine woodwork finish for the yard's fiberglass boats.

Arlene, who loves to travel, told me that for many years, Steve's boat delivery duties gave them the chance to cruise between Maine and Florida. In the 1980s, every November for six years, they delivered a boat named *Fishwife* to Florida, stayed through April in an apartment at the home of their employer, and then delivered the boat back to Northeast Harbor. "The first day of November we were out of here, come hell or high water," Arlene said.

At the Florida house one year, Arlene got a job she didn't really want. "The cook and butler decided they'd had enough of Florida," she said. A new cook came along. "But he couldn't find a butler. I wasn't doing anything, so I said, 'If there's anything I can do to help you out, I'll be glad to.' Five years later, I was still a butler. So a few jokers said, 'Well, what do we call her? A butlerette? A buttress?'"

In the 2000s, the couple took a trip to Washington, D.C., related to Spurling's war service. "What year did you go?" I ask—a routine question.

She consults with Spurling: "Do you remember what year you cut your thumb off?"

Wait. What?

"It was in the spring of 2005 because he was going like this [she sticks her thumb up] because he had a pin in it. I got his doctor to write it out on a prescription because we had to go through security when we flew." Well, we agree, at least it was a positive gesture. Thumbs up! But that all begs a certain question.

"It got caught in a table saw," he explained. "You know what? A table saw will cut your thumb just as easy as it will wood." The event resulted in another distinction for Spurling. At the time in his eighties, he was thought to be the oldest person ever to have a digit reattached. "He made medical history," Arlene said.

The couple brings out old photos. Some from the 1930s show a Cranberry Isles harbor. Spurling points out a "little bitty" boat that used to carry the mail and a few passengers for ten cents. Finally it went up to a quarter. Lobsterboats, open and narrow, look small and vulnerable compared with today's powerhouses. A photo from the 1940s shows the harbor full of ice. "We used to have to wait for an icebreaker from Portland," Spurling said. "One time, it got froze so hard that when somebody needed a doctor, they put a flat-bottom rowboat on top of a handsled, in case the ice broke, went across the Western Way and come got him and brought him to Cranberry and took him back the same way."

Arlene found a photo of *Trail Away*. After his father died, Steve bought *Trail Away* from his stepmother, used it a few years and then took the boat captain job and didn't need it. In the 1950s, Steve sold the boat. It was recently restored.

Impressed by their marriage of more than sixty years, I asked how they've been able to maintain the bliss. His partial deafness plays a role. "I say he can't hear right. He says I don't talk right," Arlene joked.

Chapter 8

RALPH AND RICHARD STANLEY

FROM LEGACY TO BEYOND

Ralph Stanley has a "local legend" vibe going on. He's an elder statesman in the wooden boatbuilding industry, a National Heritage Fellow and Boatbuilder Laureate of Maine. He's a go-to guru for the region's shipbuilding history and the community's genealogy—for which his own DNA is embedded in every line of descent possible—and he's got a wicked memory for countless names and dates. He makes fiddles, bright-varnished, with beautifully carved lion heads topping the fingerboard. He's also a big contributor to the preservation and rebirth of Friendship sloops, those gorgeous, sailing lobsterboats of the pre-motorized era and now the precious gems of a jolly bunch of sailors.

So Ralph has a live-wire thing going on. Which is odd because he's a really low-key guy who, in his eighties, is given to deliberative pauses that his listener best not interrupt if more information is forth to come. I discovered this when periodically consulting him on the old-time builders. Most recently, I brought him old Richtown boat photos to see what he knew. It turns out it's a lot. He identified boats going back eighty years, even reciting lines of ownership. One boat was named *Shearwater*; Tud Bunker sailed it for the summer people who had it built.

"Eventually, the Northeast Harbor Fleet got it and used it for a committee boat," he said. "It had an eight-cylinder engine, I think Chrysler. But the fleet took it out and gave it to my father, and he put it in his boat. It had a cracked manifold, and he patched it with liquid steel stuff and it lasted for as long as he used the boat."

Ralph Stanley rows to shore, circa 1950. *Millard Joseph Herrick photo/Ralph Warren Stanley Collection.*

Ralph can go on like this. Take Jarvis Newman's great-grandfather Henry. In the 1800s, Henry built the *Kate Newman*, which collided, loaded with stone, with a three-masted schooner loaded with lumber off the Jersey coast at night in a snowstorm and rough seas. *Kate Newman* went down, and the captain, possibly Henry's son, Everett, drowned. The only survivor got knocked or jumped onto the other schooner with the impact.

Then there are his Prohibition stories—like Customs Officer Howe Higgins finding a lobster car on the beach full of booze and charging the fisherman. But the charge didn't stick because no one could prove that the fisherman put the booze there. Or there was the guy who stuck a bottle of home-brew in his pocket while collecting pies for a Woman's Christian Temperance Union meeting. The bottle got warm, fell out of his pocket, popped the cap and sprayed the hall.

How about Oscar Krantz from Copenhagen, who worked on tramp steamers traveling the world as a youth and decided to visit his adoptive Uncle Fred on Great Cranberry? It was winter. Thinking that it would be a four-hour trip from New York, he took three successive boats, a buckboard

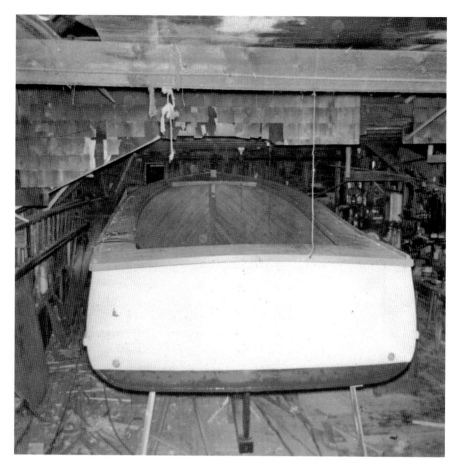

The lobsterboat built for Oscar Krantz at Ralph Stanley's shop, 1957. *Mr. and Mrs. Ralph Stanley Collection/SWHPLDA.*

and a fishing boat, arriving with frostbitten hands. He thought that fishing looked like fun. He got Charles "Dud" Bracy to cut a boat in two and add four feet in the middle to make a twenty-five-footer; used that boat a while; got Dud to build him a thirty-one- or thirty-two-footer; wore that boat out; had the Richtown brothers build him a thirty-five-footer; sold that one to his son, Emery; and then had Ralph build him a twenty-eight-footer.

Folks, this was in the 1940s and 1950s. How in the world does he remember all this stuff? Ralph chuckled. "I just remember. I used to spend a lot of time on the fish wharf, you know, listen to the stories the men told. Some of them you can't repeat." Ralph is a treasure-trove of anecdotes. But let's get to the man himself.

THROUGH HIS MOTHER, BERTHA, Ralph descended from *Mayflower* pilgrims William Brewster, Stephen Hopkins, John Howland and John Tilley. So did many other locals. "When I was a boy growing up in Southwest Harbor in my grandmother's house, there were a total of 26 *Mayflower* descendants just among our household, the houses to either side of us and the four houses across the street," he wrote for the MDI Historical Society.

Ralph also claims links to at least twenty of the area's early settlers, dating back to the mid-1700s. The Stanley family, possibly deported from England for stealing sheep, arrived in Beverly, Massachusetts, around 1640. Some continued on to Marblehead, where the dregs of society ended up. That was the Stanleys.

The Stanleys fished on the Grand Banks in the summer and made shoes in the winter. In the mid-1700s, brothers John and Sans Stanley could be found fishing off the Cranberry Isles in the summer, returning to Marblehead in the fall. By 1798, the brothers owned land on the Cranberries and lived there year-round. The MDI Stanleys descend from these two brothers.

Sans had a great-grandson named Enoch, who was Ralph's great-grandfather. Born in 1820 on Great Cranberry, Enoch grew up to command five or six large fishing schooners over the years. He was known as a smart and successful mackerel fisherman, a man of exemplary habits and frugal industry, active in the affairs of the town and holding positions of trust, which he filled conscientiously, according to a January 21, 1903 article in the *Bar Harbor Record* via Ralph Stanley.

Enoch and his wife, Caroline, had ten children, all born on Great Cranberry. The family lived on a cove called the Pool, where boats anchored and most of the island's boatbuilding was done. Old age and impaired health forced Enoch to give up command of his favorite vessel, but he still spent his late years on the water, close to shore, fishing and lobstering until his death at eighty-two in 1903.

Enoch's second-youngest child was Arno—Ralph's grandfather. Arno had a few brothers who, as Ralph's great-uncles, figure warmly in the family story. William Doane Stanley was known as Uncle Jimmy or Pa Jim. The other was Uncle Lew, the youngest. Uncle Jimmy and Uncle Lew, with their wives, Nancy and Leah, lived on Great Cranberry along the Pool. One of Uncle Lew's boathouses blew down in a storm in 1978. Today, the other boathouse is occupied by an artist's retreat. Uncle Jimmy bought fish, dressed them and drove them by sloop to J.L. Stanley and Sons of Manset. He and Aunt Nan didn't have children, but they often had one or another of their nieces and nephews living with them.

Arno was a wholesale fish dealer. He wrote a letter of proposal to a cousin, Mabel Stanley, who was raised on nearby Baker Island. "I love you with all my heart and I am willing to part with all on earth for your [presence]," he wrote, promising to "die in despair" if she rejected him. "[P]lease write on this peper and give me ether way you choose," he added, signing off, "yours Truly, Arno P. Stanley." Mabel wrote, "Yes Dear," and sent the paper back. (This charming document can be found at cranberryisles. com, the local history website curated by Bruce Komusin, who passed away in 2015.) They married in 1894, lived on Great Cranberry and had six children. One of the children was Chester, Ralph's father.

Arno turned out to be difficult. He took down the stovepipe because too much wood was being burned. He

Enoch Boynton Stanley, circa 1870. *Ralph Warren Stanley Collection/SWHPLDA.*

took a shotgun and was going to shoot his brother Lew, but he didn't. Mabel left him and returned with the children to Baker Island. Arno was committed to a state hospital in Bangor in the 1930s and died there. Ralph was eight when Arno died; he had met his grandfather only once. "He was just kind of crazy," he said. "Nowadays, they'd probably treat him with medication and he'd a been all right."

Ralph and Uncle Lew were close. It was Uncle Lew who told Ralph the story about the Boiler. In the 1890s, Enoch and all his sons had a dream to move an eleven-ton boulder from the Pool. The rock sat right in the channel, between Fish Point and the big ledge, a menace to boats going in and out. Vessels had to be awfully careful. A vessel got caught one time, said Ralph. "They had an argument what to do. My great-grandfather said to swing the vessel around and she'd come off the rocks, and they said no, she wouldn't clear Fish Point. He said she would. So they were arguing about it. Finally the tide took her, and there was nothing they could do. She swung around and she did clear Fish Point, and she came off the rock," Ralph said during a recorded SWHHS talk in 1996.

A later newspaper article credits Uncle Jimmy and others with accomplishing their long-cherished desire to move the boulder. They went out on the low drain tides and dug around the rock to break the suction. It took several years. Finally, they drilled a hole in the top, wedged in an iron bolt, put a pole across two dories and chained the assemblage to the rock at low tide, with the idea the rising tide would lift the dories and thus the rock. Both dories sank. The next time, they tried it with four dories. It was all those four dories could lift. They dragged the boulder to where they wanted to drop it and got it almost there, but the eyebolt pulled out and the dories popped out of the water. The rock sits there now. Uncle Jimmy was elated.

Chester was a boy going to school on Cranberry Island, probably getting done before he finished eighth grade so he could go fishing. For a while, like other young men on the island, he was on the crew of a Tydol oil tanker run by a Frenchman who married a Cranberry Island Stanley. Ralph remembered talking with his father about oil companies and their claims of being the best brand. "My father says, 'There's nothing to it. When Tydol was out of gas, we'd go to Standard Oil to fill up. Gas is gas,' he said. And he told about one fella—they were loading gasoline, and this guy was standing in the engine room doorway smoking a cigarette. You could see the fumes coming up by him. And my father says, 'You're going to blow us up.' 'No,' he says. 'There's plenty of air. It'll never blow.' And it didn't."

Chester wasn't interested in furthering his education, but he helped several brothers. He paid five dollars per month for room and board in Southwest Harbor so a younger brother, Leslie, could attend high school. Two other brothers, John and Robert, went to high school in Portland. Chester took John fishing with him so they could both save money to send John to the University of Maine. John later joined the Coast Guard, working the North Atlantic ice patrol. In 1943, John was in New York Harbor when a munitions ship burst into flames, threatening to cause a giant explosion that could have destroyed huge swaths of surrounding areas. It was John's first day in charge of the Staten Island Coast Guard station. He called for volunteers and led them onto the ship to attempt to douse the flames. The strategy failed, and the ship was towed to open water and sunk. Robert worked at Bath Iron Works for a while and then joined the U.S. Navy. During the war, his ship was torpedoed, and he spent quite some time in the water. Leslie went to business college and spent fifty years with a wholesale drug supplier in Portland.

Growing up, the siblings continued to take advantage of Uncle Jimmy and Aunt Nan's hospitality when the couple moved to the mainland, in Manset. Chester was there when Uncle Jimmy bought a 1924 Essex automobile for $800 and drove it around the harbor. He reached home and drove up the driveway, but when he got into the barn, he didn't know how to stop it. "My father and Aunt Nan heard a crash, and there was the Essex with the front end out through the end of the barn," Ralph said during a recorded SWHHS talk in 2008. "The wheels were still spinning, and Uncle Jimmy was standing there scratching his head. Jimmy said, 'Ches, if you can get her out, she's yours.' My father drove the car until 1936."

CHESTER WAS LIVING WITH Uncle Jimmy when he met Bertha Robinson, whose family in the area goes back to the 1790s, maybe earlier. Bertha's great-grandfather Levi and her grandfather Judson commanded good-size coasting schooners. Captain Jud—who first went to sea with his father when he was nine, steering the vessel to Boston—carried mostly lumber, coal and stone. One time, he offloaded four hundred tons of coal at the Manset Coal Company wharf. The wharf collapsed, and the business closed. "I think they salvaged most of the coal," said Ralph. "But when I was a boy, I could go down to the beach there and find pieces."

Captain Jud loved the sea, sailing along the East Coast and possibly to South America and the Caribbean. He also took time to marry, have four children and set the family up in a big house on Main Street in Southwest Harbor. His wife, Henrietta, was part of the prominent Clark Point family. Captain Jud and Henrietta's son Ralph was Ralph Stanley's grandfather. Another son, Fred, was blinded in a dynamite explosion as part of a road crew. A daughter, Lucy, was pretty deaf in old age and carried an ear trumpet. Another daughter, Bertha, gave music lessons but died young, at thirty-two. A ditty at the Southwest Harbor library, written in 1892, mentions Bertha: "Music hath power to charm and soothe the savage breast/And in giving music lessons, Bertha Robinson does her best/At organ or piano she can turn an honest penny/Thus her promised dollar has been added to the many."

As a young man, Ralph Robinson, still living with Judson and Henrietta, opened a painting business in a shop out back. He specialized in horse-drawn carriages, with gold-leaf lettering and fancy pinstripes on the wheels. "When he did one of those carriages, he'd dust for days and wouldn't let anyone in the shop. They came out perfect," Ralph Stanley said.

Robinson and the woman he would marry, Celestia "Lessie" Dix, were both children of sea captains, although Jud was a far greater success than

Lessie's father, John, who lost his vessel off Labrador and never did much after that. John's family was poor. Lessie became an excellent seamstress because the family always had to repair and remake their old clothes.

Ralph and Lessie Robinson stayed on with Judson and Henrietta, later inheriting the house. Word of Lessie's sewing skill spread to the summer people, a frugal lot who kept the same clothes at their summer homes for years, bringing them to Lessie for repair or alterations to suit changing fashions.

The Robinsons had an only child, whom they named Bertha after Ralph Robinson's sister who had died young. This Bertha went on to become a nurse, graduating from the Massachusetts General Hospital's School of Nursing, with some time off to care for her father when he was dying. Soon after graduation, Bertha married Chester Stanley. The couple moved in with Lessie and two years later had their first child, whom they named after Bertha's father. This child was Ralph Stanley. Soon, the big house was filled with seven more children, all daughters.

The family was happy but financially stretched. Young Ralph didn't see much of his father, except when he helped him on the boat. Chester spent winters fishing for lobsters. In the 1930s, he probably didn't fish more than 120 traps, and he got good wages out of that. He bought a used, no-name boat from Chester Clement and fished the boat until 1961, sometimes going thirty miles offshore in the winter and wearing out a few engines along the way, according to Ralph Stanley, recorded in an interview for the GMHH collection. Chester had a narrow escape in the winter of 1934. "Mr. Stanley was with a number of other lobster fishermen and snow, vapor and frost kept him behind until finally, with his boat tossing about with the engine stalled, he dropped anchor and spent the night on the water," a newspaper account notes. Ralph was five, and Bertha was worried sick while fishermen searched for him.

Chester made a flare by soaking rags in gasoline and lighting them in a bucket. People on shore could see his flares but didn't have a boat to get him. His boat drifted, but the anchor finally fetched up on a shoal ledge. Clarence Harding from Bass Harbor found him and towed him to Great Cranberry, where people got him warmed up.

Like many other fishermen, Chester hired himself out as a boat captain to summer families. He landed a lifelong job through Uncle Jimmy, who had Chester Clement build a thirty-one-foot open boat, named it *Leader* and chartered it out with his nephew as skipper. Until his death in 1971, Chester Stanley sailed each summer for the Neilsons, a longtime Northeast Harbor summer family.

Niliraga, 1941. *W.H. Ballard Collection/SWHPLDA.*

Bertha was mild but cheerful. Lessie did a lot of the cooking, while Bertha washed, ironed and generally cared for her growing brood. By age twelve or thirteen, Ralph was pretty happy to go off to the Manset fish wharf to earn pocket change baiting trawls while he listened to the stories the men told and hung out among the boats. He liked to design and build model boats and airplanes. At eighteen, thanks to Uncle Lew's connection as a boat captain with the wealthy Dunn and Milliken summer families of Northeast Harbor, Ralph got a summer job as a cook aboard the family schooner, *Niliraga*. That helped pay for tuition, something like $600 per year, at Ricker Junior College in Houlton, where he majored in liberal arts and graduated penniless. "Scholarships weren't floating around like they are today," he said. "I probably would have gone further in school if I'd had more money."

Ralph was twenty-two and moved back in with his parents, who still had a house full of kids. Living rent-free, with his grandfather's paint shop available out back, Ralph decided to try building a twenty-eight-foot lobsterboat for himself. After a summer of earnings to pay for materials, he set to work,

Ralph Stanley's first lobsterboat, 1953. *Ralph Warren Stanley Collection/SWHPLDA.*

getting it half-done until the next summer, when he made more money for more materials and a down payment on an engine.

"Got it in the water and I thought, 'I'm glad that's over with,'" he said. "I thought I would never have the courage to start another one." Two months later, Dick Yates, a Foreign Service officer who summered in Southwest Harbor, came along and asked for a boat. Illness and many months in the hospital interrupted the start of Ralph's career. But he quickly picked up where he left off, splitting the year for the next two decades between building boats in the winter and skippering *Niliraga* summers.

Ralph's career is well documented, particularly in Craig Milner's terrific *Ralph Stanley: Tales of a Maine Boatbuilder* (2004). Roger Duncan's *Dorothy Elizabeth: Building a Traditional Wooden Schooner Paperback* (2000) gets into specifics of a particular boat. There's also Hope Wurmfeld's *Boatbuilder* (1988) and Jeff Dobbs's 2015 documentary *Ralph Stanley: An Eye for Wood.*

Milner chronicled Ralph's four decades on the job, tallying about seventy boats in all, from schooners and sloops to lobsterboats and lobster-style pleasure boats, many still seen in local waters. His first sailboat, the Friendship sloop *Hieronymus*, came out in 1962.

A succession of lobsterboats followed. In 1973, he rebuilt the 1904 Friendship sloop *Dictator* and built a sloop for Ed Kaelber, the first president

The twenty-eight-foot lobsterboat *Betty Lou*, built in 1958. *Ralph Warren Stanley Collection/ SWHPLDA.*

Hieronymous, 1962. Mr. and Mrs. Ralph Stanley Collection/SWHPLDA.

of College of the Atlantic. Kaelber's help enabled Ralph to build a new shop on the Southwest Harbor shore, next to Uncle Jimmy's house, which he inherited from his father. From then on, his career turned largely toward Friendship sloops and other pleasure craft.

Ralph had known a young lady named Marion Linscott since they were kids, although Ralph was several years older. Later on, they started dating, and that was about it. They married in 1956 and produced a family of four children, enjoying boat outings, picnics and visits to friends.

From a young age, it became clear that their son Richard had inherited his father's boatbuilding ways. Ralph would later wonder if he'd done the right thing to encourage his son. But Richard had zero doubts. "When I was a little kid, I just wanted to be with my father all the time, and I wanted to be a boatbuilder. That's all I wanted to do," Richard said. "So I was with him as much as I could be."

Now in his fifties, Richard is a tall man with a thatch of graying hair, gray stubble and a gruff voice that fetches up deep in his throat. His back is hunched, his gait is stiff and his eyes have a preoccupied look. All traits combined give the initial impression that he's taciturn. He's not. He's a sweet guy and a great storyteller. One of his stories is a corker. At seventeen, he was a backseat passenger when the car he was in spun out on black ice, hitting a tree, another car and a telephone pole. He broke his second, third and fourth vertebrae but didn't realize he was injured. He got out to walk home. "I was rubbing my neck, going, 'Oh, my f---ing neck. I gotta go home. I'm hungry,'" he recalled. "My cousin chased me down the road and convinced me to come back because he could see there was something really wrong."

He woke up in the hospital, his head immobilized. "I didn't know anything, why I was there, what had happened. I was freaking out, with this bar around my head. I was, like, 'I'm getting out of here.' So I reached up and started pulling it off, but I couldn't get the tips of the bolts out of the side of my head." He mimed himself struggling then laughed. "Oh god, that hurt! And before I know it, I'm surrounded and pinned to the bed, and they're taking this bar off and they've stuck these sandbags around my head and I was freaking out. 'Man, this is not right! Let me go!' They got this new bar 'cause I bent that one. They started tightening them bolts. I'm, like, 'Holy frig!' The pressure those bolts make. Does that hurt! And they didn't use the same holes! They made new ones!"

He continued, "I was livid, man! They sedated me then. When I came to, there was this girl in this wheelchair who had been all stove up in a Trans Am T-top that had rolled over I don't know how many times. She broke almost every bone in her body. She was there because they wanted someone to calmly tell me why I was there. I was all cast and bandages, but she was a nice-looking girl. I say, 'Oh, I've gone to heaven!'"

Doctors took bone from his hip, drilled, straightened, wired and chinked. He laughed. "I could have done the operation myself, you know. They were just using tools that I use—stainless steel nails and wires, twist them up like bread ties and get the right tension on them."

ALTHOUGH HE HAS A wild background from his younger years, Richard is mostly all about wooden boats, thanks to the passion he inherited from Ralph. From age five or six, Richard loved being out back at his father's first shop. Unbidden, Richard happily scrubbed bottoms, swept shavings, knocked in bungs, greased the ways and did some sanding. "I'd be up there as often as I could, pretty much every day," he said. "And that little shop, every day, was cold and narrow and dark. He built one forty-four-foot lobsterboat in that barn. He had to pull it outdoors and put the top on." He laughed. "They had *Playboy* centerfolds all along the walls. Gee, I loved that."

The planer sat at the front of the shop, and a little door was cut into the wall at the height of the planer, with a hinged cover over it. "You could send things through the planer inside, and unless it was a short piece, you had to go outside and retrieve it from the outside and shove it back through. But it worked."

As Richard got older, their relationship could be frustrating. He always admired his father's talents and still goes to him for advice occasionally. But as a kid, there were many times when he was eager to dive into the next stage of learning, long before he was actually allowed to. "I was using the bandsaw at my junior high shop class before I was allowed to use the bandsaw at my father's shop," he said. "He was very cautious, always worried about me getting my hand crushed or cut."

So he learned by watching. "My father had a crew that had been with him numerous years," Richard noted. "I would watch them. I also went to other yards. I'd stay back, out of the way, and watch. And when I saw an opportunity to help, I would, as long as I wasn't going to be in their way."

Southwest Boat was just down the road. "They'd be working down there on various types of boats," he recalled. "They were doing a lot of repair work on sardine carriers and things like that. I'd go down there, and they'd be tearing these big bows of these sardine carriers apart and putting on new stems and forefoots and new deck pieces and tearing out the sterns and everything. I would watch the guys doing that."

The lobsterboat *Frances Inez*, built in 1968. *Ralph Warren Stanley Collection/SWHPLDA.*

He remembered going down to Jimmy Rich's. "They were building a powerboat over there one time, and they had just got the rabbet all cut and chiseled out. And they were sandpapering it! They were sandpapering a rabbet! And I was like, 'Wow, I've never seen that before!' That's how fussy Jimmy Rich was about building boats."

At a machine shop where his father had metal fittings made, Richard remembered "great big lathes and milling machines and all this junk everywhere, and just a little path through there and a little area to work at the machine. Otherwise it was just stacked with metal junk. You'd go in there and ask Father Power for something, and Father Power would go to his junk, and he knew right where everything was. He had a few fingers missing, you know. He'd dig around and he'd pull it out, and there it is! It was really fun to go to places like that."

Once in a while, he got to visit Raymond Bunker at the Bunker and Ellis shop in Manset. One time, when Richard was in high school, Bunker popped into Ralph's shop:

I was making this half-model of a powerboat. At the time, Raymond Bunker was still building boats. I don't know why he came over, but he comes in and he sees me sanding on my half-model. And he says [Stanley adopts a big, gruff voice], *"Let me see that, sonny!" So I let him have it. He looks at it. He says, "Huh! It's too wide! Got the right idea though!" Another time, he comes in and I was working away—this was later on after he retired. He comes in, chewing his pipe, and stands around looking. He'd ask Ralph a few questions—"How much deadrise to that sheer you got?"—you know, stuff like that. And he'd be watching me. And he says, "Ralph, you have a few more boys like that, you won't have to work!" Another day, Raymond comes in. I'm left-handed, and I was painting a boat and he sees I'm using my left hand to paint. And he says, "Sonny!"… He's in his eighties, so I guess he had the right to call me sonny…He says, "Sonny! You're putting that paint on backwards!"*

As he got older, Richard learned a lot from taking apart derelict boats and repairing and rebuilding the many wooden lobsterboats the older generation had at the time. He recalled taking out bow planks from a Bunker and Ellis boat. "I couldn't believe what I saw," he laughed. "The forward floor timber was square. It wasn't beveled. The forward edge fit against the planking, and the rest of it was just all gap. I said, 'My God, this boat's how old here, and there's never been any problem with that? There ain't no sense doing what we've been doing!' But then it comes time for me to put the floor timbers in. I think about that, and I'm saying, 'Eh, I guess I'd better fit it.'"

Graduating from the Boat School in Eastport in 1982, Richard began receiving a name credit in his father's business a year later, with the construction of the schooner *Equinox*. In 1986, he acquired a quarter interest in the business. "One time, we got a Friendship sloop planked up, and my father says, 'Well, the boat needs the interior'—and he leaves," Richard recalled. "So—there my interior career started. I went and looked at the other boats. I'd watched him do it before. And I went from there. Now [he let loose a wry chuckle], was that the most efficient way to learn how to do that? Probably not. But probably it stuck with me a lot better."

If it sounds like he worked a lot, he did. "There were years there I did a lot of partying. But I was still there to work." He laughed. "I was always waiting for the police to come."

Gradually, he became the shop boss, teaching many employees over the years. "A guy off the street is usually much more teachable than a guy who has worked at other yards or a guy who's gone to a boat school because they know the way they've been taught," he said. "Whereas there can be twelve different ways to do things in boatbuilding. I've done most of these twelve different things, and I know which one works the best and gives me the results I'm looking for. Other people are looking for other results and other ways can work better for them. But in my shop, you've got to do it this way. And it can be a hard for people to accept. So you have to retrain them. But if you get someone of the street, they're more apt to listen to you."

In the age of fiberglass and composites, wooden boatbuilding has its ups and downs, Richard said. He recalled a surge of interest in the 1970s, when the idea of building wooden boats had a romantic aura for back-to-the-landers. "It looks romantic from the outside, but it's a lot of hard work," he said. "You have to use a lot of awful chemicals. White lead paste is toxic, and there are lots of different paints and chemicals. So that back-to-nature thing was not quite what it looked like. That renaissance of wooden boatbuilders kind of died off."

Richard met a young woman named Lorraine in 2000 when he was fixing the rudder post box on her father's tourboat. Lorraine has big, beautiful eyes set in a pixie face and a boyish physique, and she gives the impression of running on high-octane energy. After college and office jobs in New York, she went to work for her father. Apparently, Richard's presence was something of an event. "It was, 'Oh, we've got Richard Stanley coming!'" she said. "So I was, like, 'Who is this guy? What is up?'"

"I see this young lady walking around, and I thought she was attractive," Richard continued. "At the end of the day, her father and she were together, and we just started talking. I started telling them about how I was building this little Friendship sloop for myself, and I was going to work on it that evening. And she showed up with a tin of cookies."

"Well, you invited us by for a tour," said Lorraine.

"Well, I remember I invited you for a tour. But that evening you just came over."

"That might have been Monday evening."

"I remember it was that evening."

"Well, anyway, it was pretty quick."

"It was pretty quick."

It was oatmeal chocolate chip cookies—Rosemary's recipe from Frankie's diner. "I felt quite lucky to get it from her," said Lorraine.

"So then, 'cause them cookies were really good, we just got along," Richard said with a mischievous smile.

All summer long, Lorraine had noticed a beautiful boat in the harbor. "I thought it was the prettiest boat out there. They said, 'That's Richard

Richard Stanley, circa 2010. *Laurie Schreiber.*

Stanley,'" she said. "He seemed to know who he was and what he was doing and why he was doing it. And you could either like it or not."

Lorraine continued to visit Richard at Ralph's shop. "I asked him if he wanted any help—knowing absolutely nothing about boatbuilding," she said. Just like that, he took her on. Since then, she's been instrumental in helping Richard move from the Ralph W. Stanley brand to Richard Stanley Custom Boats. These days, he takes care of many of the boats built under the Ralph W. Stanley name and is also marketing a new kind of boat—a comfortable wood hull with an easy-maintenance fiberglass top.

"I love wooden boatbuilding because I have a way to be able to imagine the finished product before it's done, before it even begins," Richard said. "I can see that boat all finished. What I love to do mostly is build keels. If I could just do one thing in life, I would be a wooden-boatbuilding keel-making fool. I just like doing that. I like working those big pieces of wood, and I like cutting the rabbets and timber gains and shaping it. I like doing that. My father liked to plank the boats. I like planking boats, too. I like lining up the planks and making the plank lines come out nice and looking right."

It's the artist in him. "I just like creating, and I think wooden boats are beautiful. I think they feel good in the water under your feet. They are dead wood, but they're so alive. They have my life in them, my eye and my life, my feel, and that's what I like. I love to create and build the boat. But what I really like is seeing them being used. These people who say, 'Oh, this boat is too beautiful to be used!' Noooo! Don't hurt me—use it!"

Chapter 9

DINNER WITH THE HINCKLEYS

HOW FAMILY, CREW AND CULTURE MADE A WORLD-CLASS BRAND

Gwen Hinckley practically had a bed-and-breakfast going for the clients, friends and tradespeople associated with the boatbuilding firm of her husband, Henry Rose Hinckley II. "If you were able to find some of the old customers, they'd laugh about staying with Henry and Gwen," said Hank Hinckley, their youngest child. "Dad would get up and go to bed at 8:30 p.m. If we were still at the dinner table, it didn't make any difference. The president could be sitting there, and he'd go up and go to bed. Mom would do her best to carry on the conversation. That's probably how Bob got to be a good salesman. He'd have to pick up the conversation. Us kids would be [amazed look], 'Dad's gone! He's just gone!' But you could catch him on his way out at 4:30 a.m. in the morning. He'd get up, have zwieback and milk. Then he'd rattle around some, and off he'd go to work. I'd roll over and go back to sleep."

Recently, Hank was at his boat shop, not far from the Hinckley yard, refurbishing several yachts with his crew and a young apprentice. I had swung in to ask Hank warm and fuzzy questions about his family, which was not a warm and fuzzy family but rather rock-solid and certainly exciting in many ways. An approachable guy prone to itemizing all his professional misadventures ("I've cut things three or four times and they're still too short") while praising everyone around him, Hank started hanging out at his father's yard, occasionally "working" with his dad in the glass shop, when he was eight. "For a kid, it's an ideal way to grow up, if you like boats," he said.

Back in the day, his dad's yard opened at seven o'clock, but guys were down there at five o'clock in the morning, banging out ideas. "There was incredible skill—not just hand skill, but talent and engineering and design—and a lot of it happened sitting under the cradles in the morning. Dad wouldn't miss those morning meetings because those guys would talk about ideas and problems they had, and they'd solve them there. The design crew went a lot farther than the third floor of the office. Dad would throw in a concept, and it would get banged around, and couple of days later, it'd be fine-tuned and it'd be in a boat."

THERE WAS ONCE A GOOD chance that the Hinckley company might have gone under a different name. In the early nineteenth century, the name almost died out. One generation lacked male children. But a daughter promised her father that one of her sons would adopt the name. So when he came of age, Samuel Hinckley Lyman became Samuel Lyman Hinckley. Samuel married Henrietta Rose, and they had an only child, Henry Rose Hinckley, a Civil War officer who went to law school but ended up in the cutlery trade. (Most information herein about the family's time in Northampton and early days in Manset comes from the 1997 work *The Hinckley Story* by Benjamin Barrett Hinckley Jr.)

Henry settled down in Northampton and married Mary Barrett, the daughter of Dr. Benjamin Barrett, who owned one of Northampton's oldest houses, called the Manse. Henry and Mary lived in the Manse and raised six children. One was named Benjamin, who went into Henry's cutlery business and married Agnes Chamberlin Childs, who became a physics teacher at Smith. As today's descendants understand it, Agnes may have done some engineering with the Wright brothers on their flying machines.

Ben and Agnes had four children—Henry Rose Hinckley II, Frances (Franna), Benjamin Jr. and George—and turned the Manse into an inn while also keeping up with the cutlery business. In 1924, it was time for a vacation. Ben Sr. knew Manset from his college years, when a group of buddies spent the summer there. They rented a cottage and then bought a summer home, which they named the Moorings. Next door was a little business for boat storage and repairs. It used to be a fish wharf in the 1880s and 1890s, belonging to James Parker, who, with his four sons, "developed the largest wholesale fish business in Maine, with a fleet of 15 to 20 vessels, about 150 men, and distributing about $100,000 in payroll annually. During this period, fish curing and canning businesses in Manset and Bass Harbor were flourishing," as was the summer resort industry, according to *Mount*

The building between the two masts is James Parker's shed. *Ralph Warren Stanley Collection/SWHPLDA.*

Desert Island: Somesville, Southwest Harbor, and Northeast Harbor by Earle G. Shettleworth Jr. and Lydia B. Vandenbergh.

After Parker's death, the wharf ended up in the hands of Erasmus "Hans" Hansen, a Swedish sailmaker, who stored and repaired boats and constructed a marine railway. A bachelor, he drank too much and would be out of commission two weeks at a time. By 1927, Hans was ready to quit. His retirement was short-lived. He got drunk, fell off the wharf and drowned.

"So my grandfather had to start running the damned place," said Bob, Henry and Gwen's oldest child. "He said, 'Well, okay, the boats are here. We'll launch them in the spring, and then I'm tearing the business down. That's the end of it.' Nobody in the family had any intention of going into the boat business. He ran it for a year or so. Everything was a dollar. An hour's labor was a dollar, a can of varnish was a dollar, a can of bottom paint was a dollar. He had it very simple."

Growing up in Northampton and shipped off to boarding schools, Henry was bright and independent-minded but averse to formal education. He liked mechanical things, automobiles, planes, crystal radio receivers and engines. He was into photography and developed his own prints. He liked camping, canoeing and fishing in remote areas. He studied mechanical aeronautical engineering at the University of Cincinnati, took flight training, secured his pilot's license, eventually owned his own plane and then spent several years studying at Cornell.

Bob recalled that his father also designed and tested airplane instruments for a while. "In those days, you take an instrument, you frig with it, you put it in, you take it up and fly it and see if it worked," Bob said. No one stayed with that job. Henry soon found out why. "They had a lot of crashes," said Bob. "You'd take off in this rattletrap, and a lot of times, you couldn't get back to the runway. You'd land in fields and all kinds of things. This Ford Trimotor was a big airplane. He was flying that thing and landed somewhere and a wheel broke. He had to get out and jack it up, and it fell on him. They came along and got him out. He was really lucky."

In 1932, Henry was twenty-five and had finished his studies at Cornell. The Depression had hit its peak and was about to turn. Henry and Ben Jr. were scrambling for ways to make money. They headed to Manset, Henry to run the boatyard and Ben Jr. to turn the Moorings into an inn. Soon, Henry was building his first craft, a thirty-six-foot fishing/charter boat named *Ruthyeolyn*, trimmed in Philippine mahogany. The family presumes that Henry designed the boat, perhaps with input from others.

Henry met a young lady named Gwen, who had a wonderful personality that triumphed over adverse circumstances during her childhood. She was born to Margaret and Ervin Bracy, who also had twin boys. Gwen was six when the influenza pandemic of 1919 struck. It killed her mother and one of her infant brothers; the other brother was rendered deaf.

Ervin traveled quite a bit as a salesman for the Standard Oil Company of New York, so Gwen and her little brother spent much of their early lives with their mother's relatives in New Brunswick. In high school, she moved to Southwest Harbor to be with her father's family. At twenty-one, she met Henry, a good-looking young man of twenty-seven whose up-and-coming business provided some stability after the hardships of the Depression. They married in 1934 without fanfare, and babies started coming straightaway: Bob, Edward (Bud), Ann, Jane and Hank. In 1939, they moved to a nice Victorian house at the head of the harbor. Gwen was happy as a mother and housewife, with a little golf, painting and canasta thrown in. She had lots of

Henry Hinckley (left) with Winston Stewart, Howe Higgins, George Gilley, Carlton Hill and Bink Sargent, at Southwest Boat. *W.H. Ballard photo/David Sargent Collection/SWHPLDA.*

friends and a busy social life through Henry, who often brought folks home on the spur of the moment. They loved to sail together.

"Gwen was a really strong person, physically and emotionally," said Bob's wife, Tina.

"Oh, yeah, very stable," said Bob. "Had to be, to live with my father."

"Henry was crazy, in a way," offered Tina.

"…like a genius," Bob noted.

"…running around, all over the place. She raised the kids and saved the money and kept everything going. This was before the age when women felt they had to fulfill themselves in other ways. She was Mrs. Henry Hinckley, and she enjoyed it."

Unlike Gwen, Henry was not a warm kind of guy. He was difficult and exciting. Bob recalled playing with the family's train set with his brother Bud when their father suddenly slammed open the door to his darkroom and flung out trays of prints. "Whirr! Crash! He had a wicked temper, and these things just came scaling out. We ducked and got out of there."

But Henry took his role as provider seriously. The kids had everything they needed, and he took them water-skiing, hunting and fishing. Winters, he flooded the backyard, and the family had skating parties. He was a great cook. Sunday popovers were a specialty. "Whenever we went sailing offshore, doing a delivery trip, he would cook," Hank recalled. "Usually, the first night out, we'd have potatoes and a roast, cooked on the boat. That was his thing. It was a nice part about cruising with Dad."

Henry had a series of small planes—a Stinson Flying Station Wagon, a Piper Tripacer, an Aero-Craft Aero-Coupe and a Cessna 182—and some pretty fancy cars. "During World War II, we had the farm up in Otis, and he had a big Packard, big god-damned thing," said Bob. "I remember getting seasick in that thing. Hated sitting in the back."

It was probably in the Packard that Henry drove Bob at high-speed to Portland for an emergency operation. "He picked up a pretty good-sized police escort on the way down," Bob said. "They finally got him pulled over. He said, 'This kid is going to die if I don't get him to the hospital!' 'All right, sir. Go ahead.' But that was the old man. He flew fast, drove fast, drank hard, smoked hard, a hundred miles an hour all the time. Nobody could keep up with him. My mother used to shake her head, 'There he goes again!'"

Crusty old coot that he was, Henry inspired devotion in his crew, not least because he would do anything to keep them employed. He had them build at least a couple of yachts on spec when the yard was out of work. "He hawked everything in the world," Hank said. "He knew he could not lose the talent in the shop. He'd drive my mother nuts. We'd sell everything. And the key guys knew he'd do that. And it was reciprocated."

One of the things Henry sold, behind her back, was Gwen's boat. Hank was a young teen when she bought *Gitana*. He recalled living with his folks on the boat one winter in Florida. "It had all the china and the old, velvet cushions and a great back porch," he said. "It was all varnish and brass and bronze. One of my jobs in the morning was to polish."

But Henry needed money at the yard. "It was some time before my mother forgave him. Admittedly, we needed a boat like that like we needed a hole in the head." That sort of scenario played out more than once in their marriage. Said Hank, sardonically, "It was always fun to listen to the two of them."

FROM EARLY ON, HENRY was forging seminal relationships with exciting young designers of the day and well-off clients, as well as developing ancillary operations. A stickler for quality and honesty and an outgoing person who enjoyed schmoozing over drinks—these traits helped build his reputation and made him a superb salesman. "Customers loved him because he was a great storyteller," said Bob. "He always felt that he could 'do it.' He could run a lathe really well, he did his own photography, he worked with other

A Hinckley Islander. *W.H. Ballard photo/SWHPLDA.*

designers, he could run this, that and the other thing. He marched to his own drum, and nobody gave him any crap. He was the kingpin."

During the first few years, the new yard built power pleasure boats and launches, up to forty-two feet. Sparkman & Stephens, founded in 1930, was making its name as an influential firm. In 1938, Hinckley had it design a thirty-foot sloop, called the *Islander*. Twenty were produced, making them the company's first mass-production line.

In 1938, Hinckley partnered with Lennox "Bink" Sargent, a distant in-law, to buy a second boatyard on the opposite side of the harbor. The Southwest Boat Corporation became a major player in the design and construction of large fishing boats and transport vessels.

The second yard came in handy when World War II came along. Hinckley jumped on the opportunity to build boats for the armed services, traveling to Washington to nail down contracts. "During World War II, he was phenomenal," said Bob. "Worked his ass off, got a lot of business for the area."

For two years, Henry and Bink had nonstop production at the two yards. By the end of the war, they and their crews had become star builders for

War boats at the Hinckley yard. *W.H. Ballard photo/SWHPLDA.*

the state of Maine, having produced 535 boats—mine yawls, tow yawls, aircraft personnel boats, picket boats and lifeboats for the army, navy and Coast Guard. The two yards received the first combined Army-Navy E, for excellence, ever conferred in Maine.

Henry sometimes told stories about those trips to the War Department. "Apparently, the guy who awarded a lot of the bids would sit down, open his lower drawer and there'd be a Coke bottle in there full of liquor," Hank said.

During those same years, Henry started a marine supply distribution company, additional storage facilities and a lumber supply yard. Ben Jr. joined the company in 1940, tended to business administration and began a boat insurance business, while Henry oversaw boatbuilding operations.

The yard remained busy after the war, building sailboats, powerboats and custom craft, including the last wooden yachts the yard would build. But Henry had seen the future, and it was fiberglass. "He wasn't unique in that thinking, by any means," said Hank. "I think a lot of people decided to go to glass about the same time, for the same reasons. And as we went into glass, a lot more people could afford boats than could before."

In the 1950s, Henry began designing and building fiberglass dinghies to study the process. He made his great leap forward when William Tripp, another early experimenter, designed the yawl that would become the

Hinckley's yard during war production. *W.H. Ballard photo/SWHPLDA.*

Venturer on the ways, the largest wooden sailboat built by Hinckley, 1961. *W.H. Ballard photo/SWHPLDA.*

Hinckley's Bermuda 40 *Jaan*, 1965. *W.H. Ballard photo/SWHPLDA.*

Bermuda 40. The first B40, named *Huntress*, debuted in 1960. It was a turning point for the company.

Hank was ten. He remembers being aboard *Huntress* with the owner, his dad and perhaps Bob, who would have been twenty-five and by that time stepping up as lead salesman. "They launched it to sea trial her," Hank said. "That was the first real Hinckley sailboat. She was a jump. We built custom boats before—*Osprey*, *Saga*—that were really nice wood boats. But Hinckley went from being Chevys, in wood, to more like a Cadillac or Rolls. When we went to glass, we shifted gear."

HENRY WAS CONSTANTLY TINKERING, looking for ways to make the next boat better than the last. For his own use, he built a couple of Sou'westers, in wood and fiberglass, and two or three B40s. All were named *Jaan*—combining the names of his daughters. "He would build his boats as a way to experiment with making them better," Hank said. "He would take one of his boats out for the weekend. He'd come back with a notebook full of ideas, and he'd rip off seven or eight pages and hand them to Herschel Norwood at the dock to see the little stuff got done. Then he'd wander up to Russell Dolliver, who ran the machine shop, and they'd commiserate a while. Then they'd come down and pull something off the boat and take it up to the machine shop to be welded and redone and put on the next weekend, and then he'd go out and try it again. It was hell trying to get the production work done."

The rugged, monocoque nature of fiberglass, and the repeatability and cost-efficiency of the process, appealed to Henry. It also allowed his skilled workers to concentrate on interiors and finish work. The hull styles and finish made Hinckley yachts stand out far more than other fiberglass boats of the day. "There are a lot of really gorgeous glass boats now," said Hank. "Not so much back then. Initially, Hinckleys really stood out in the styling and the way they were finished off."

Other production boats came on line. The process required major investments to manufacture plugs and molds. Hinckley, relying on his reputation for the yard's preceding work (many customers were repeats from the yard's wooden boat days), was able to line up orders before work had begun.

Some employees were concerned about the new material. "People just didn't want to work with it," Hank said. "It's not hard to understand—the smell, the itchiness. As I recall, there were people who wouldn't come to work for a while. They didn't want to be around the stuff. The place didn't empty out, by any means, but there were a lot of people afraid of it."

In the early days, getting the resin mixed right involved experimentation. "He'd mix this and he'd mix that; it would go smoking off," Hank said. "I wasn't there when it happened, but I guess they burned the darn place down, pretty much. It wasn't such a controlled process. It would get hot and ignite. Today, you have to get pretty far off for that to happen. But back then, it was almost common."

"All those chemicals," mused Bob. "We had a fire a week down there."

One Sunday, Henry and Bink were laying up a little outboard. Bink had to go home for Sunday dinner. "So Dad said, 'I'll finish up. You leave the beer,'" Hank related. "Dad sat down and had a beer, then finished up, then sat back down and had a couple more beers, then tried to get up. He was stuck. His pants were stuck down." Catalyst added to resin generates heat, which makes it harden. "He'd had so much to drink he didn't feel the warmth. He had to cut his pants. That's the kind of thing that went on in that back room."

BOB STARTED AT THE YARD when he was twelve or so, summers in the late '40s, cleaning boats and running errands. He became an employee in 1960, at twenty-five. He loved the life. As vice-president in charge of sales for many years, the culture of client care came naturally to him. "I'd go fishing with a customer, down east, out to one in the morning, selling a boat. We'd come back with Atlantic salmon," he said. "It's a seductive business to get into."

Bud, the middle son, was involved with the company for many years and eventually became vice-president in charge of production. Hank started at age eleven as a dock attendant and rigger in the summer of 1960. When he finished school, he started a boat business in Florida, joined the navy as a Seabee during the Vietnam War and then went back to Hinckley to work on the shop floor, working his way through the various departments. "You'd come in and find me, likely as not, with a grinder in my hand, covered in glass. No protective stuff on other than glasses. That's me. Bob is the salesman. He's the one who cleans up pretty good. Bud was technical—computers, accounting—he was strong with that. I was the nuts and bolts. I was the guy they kept in the backroom building boats, happy as a clam."

Hank became purchasing agent and manager, went to work for the Glastron Boat Company, rejoined Hinckley and became production manager and, eventually, president. In 1978, he left Hinckley to found Ocean Cruising Yachts and now runs Hank Hinckley Boat Builders.

Some combination of children might have met the approval of many parents looking for someone to take over the business. But Henry wasn't amenable to having his sons take over. Said Hank, "It should have worked. But we just drove Dad nuts. We clearly did. I think he'd had all he wanted by the time he sold out."

In 1969, Bob broke off to buy, with Tina, the old Sim Davis boatyard in Bass Harbor and run it as a storage and service yard called Bass Harbor Marine. Ben, Bob and Tina founded the Hinckley Yacht Brokerage Company a few years later.

Around the same time, Henry and Gwen started spending more time each winter in Florida. But toward the end of his life, he wasn't well. "He was having episodes of passing out," said Hank. "I can remember him and Mom being at the Seawall Dining Room, and he starts coughing. He passes out, face in the soup. Everybody went nuts. Mom pulled the soup away and said, 'No, don't touch him. He'll be back in a second.' And he would be. She got used to it after a while."

His choking fits and faints were due to a medical condition, and his heavy drinking and smoking probably exacerbated it. When he crashed his car, it's thought he was probably choking and passed out. "Dad was just gone in an instant," Hank said. "It had only been two years since he'd sold the company. I don't know if that was good, bad or whatever. But for him it was probably good. The company was his life. It was his baby."

IT WAS 1980. GWEN fared well (she died in 2005). She was pretty independent, had family to help her out and was not unaccustomed to being on her own, given Henry's work and travel schedule. Plus, she was a great investor. "She bought Chrysler at the bottom and sold it at the top," said Hank. "She managed the same through a couple of cycles with the Ford Motor Company. She'd often outperform my brother and uncle."

Two years later, Bob and a longtime friend, Shepard McKenney, later joined by John Marshall, bought back the company. "I didn't really want to buy it back," said Bob. "But there was some pressure—'What's going to happen to it?'"

"When Bob got into the business, he ran it like a business, not like an artistic endeavor," said Tina. "He brought in people who were business-oriented. His style had to be completely different from his father because his father was artistic, creative, innovative…but not such a businessman. Henry would make five dollars and go buy something with it…"

"…another airplane, an expensive car," added Bob.

In 1994, the company released the stylish and innovative jet-drive Picnic Boat, designed by Bruce King. It was the first time water jet propulsion, found previously on jet skis and ocean liners, was used on pleasure boats. It became phenomenally popular. "It was Shep's idea, but Bob took it and marketed it," said Hank. "Bob and Shep made that company click way better, in terms of size and profitability, than we ever did as a family."

In keeping with Henry's complex personality, Bob and Tina have conflicting ideas about whether his brilliance would have survived in today's world. For starters, could he have lived with today's environmental regulations? What about all those seat-of-the-pants (literally), incendiary lab experiments? "He just did what he wanted to do," said Tina, "and people did what he asked them to do: 'We need to work all night building this boat.' People just did it."

But Bob invokes the 2013 America's Cup, when four teams used catamarans with hydrofoils that allowed the hulls to lift off the water. "My father would have loved that!" he said. "That's where the aeronautical side came in. He actually would have loved the jetboats, too. He really was up here [Bob raises his hand to the stratosphere]—kind of alone, in a way."

Chapter 10
BINK SARGENT NAVIGATES A DIVERSE CAREER

In 1937, Lennox Ledyard "Bink" Sargent took a break from his studies in engineering at Harvard University, and from his summer internships with Boston naval architect A. Loring Swazey, to work for Henry Hinckley, a distant in-law who was expanding the boatyard in Manset.

Sargent was a young man of twenty with a lot of money (by local standards) and a fondness for expensive, fast cars—a bit of a hell-raiser and playboy, although his son, David Sargent, noted:

> *But that really doesn't define him, and it would be missing the point to dwell too much on that aspect of his character, colorful as it may be. He was a highly intelligent man with an encyclopedic knowledge of boats and their designs and history. He had been fascinated by boats from his early childhood, almost to the point of obsession, according to his sister, and had a lifetime of experience, ranging from extended cruises on family yachts to visits with his dad to famous boatyards and designers like Alden and Herreshoff. He was certainly a workaholic. His sister said that, as a boy, when visiting other yachts, Bink always ignored the owners and headed directly for the captain and crew, badgering them with technical questions about the boat, the design, where she was built, and why, why, why. I doubt there were many people in the industry who knew more about boats and their design and building.*

Sargent was dubbed "Binky" as a boy by his younger sister, Cynthia. "I don't know how a guy gets to be seventy-three years old and still

Bonaventure, under construction in 1942. *W.H. Ballard photo/David Sargent Collection/SWHPLDA.*

called Bink," said David. "But you know, there were tons of funny nicknames then."

David, who is retired from an international electronics firm and lives in New Hampshire, has a summer home in Tremont. He was in town one week in October to finish closing up the house for the winter and to swap photos with Charlotte Morrill and Meredith Hutchins, the lead gurus of the Southwest Harbor Public Library Digital Archive. "He had a great, offbeat sense of humor and found humor everywhere," David noted, settling into Morrill's living room. "He was a good storyteller and had lots of friends. Bobby and Roger Rich were among his friends, as were most of the other boatbuilders in the area."

Sargent was born in 1916 to Ledyard Worthington and Etta Ruth (Lennox) Sargent in Cambridge, Massachusetts. His grandfather was Dudley Allen Sargent, born in Belfast, Maine, a fitness enthusiast who founded the Sargent School of Physical Education in Cambridge in 1881. Dudley emphasized training for all students, "even weak and disabled individuals," according to the school's website.

Dudley's only child, Ledyard, took over the school when his father died in 1924. Ledyard and Etta moved in upper-class circles in Cambridge and

Martha's Vineyard. But Bink "was probably the most classless person I've known," said David. "To him, people were people and he judged them on actions, not wealth or social status."

When Bink arrived in Manset, Henry had just nailed down his first volume production of sailboats. Bink probably started out in design and worked as a trainee. He also had family wealth behind him. Henry was expanding the business and looking at ancillary opportunities. The C.E. Clement Boatyard, on the shore near Clark Point, became available due to Clement's untimely death in an automobile accident in 1937. David said that it was probably Henry who had the idea to buy the yard, drafting Bink to put up the money.

FROM THE MID-1800s, Clark Point was the scene of lively development. The southernmost tip of the peninsular bulge that comprises the core of Southwest Harbor, the point and the road leading along the shore are named after the Clark family, the predominant landowners for many years.

Sim Mayo,
circa 1905.
Jane Wilkinson
Morehouse
Collection/
SWHPLDA.

Sim Mayo's boat and mechanical shop, circa 1905. *Jane Wilkinson Morehouse Collection/SWHPLDA.*

The family built a wharf at the point, encouraging steamboat traffic, the fish trade, summer tourism and the development of businesses to support the burgeoning activity. Within this bustle lived Simeon Holden "Sim" Mayo, who was into everything.

Mayo sold and repaired boats, bicycles and engines; sold boat and automobile supplies, plumber's and gas fitter's supplies and waterworks supplies; operated a carriage shop with his brother, Dudley; and smithed metal, according to information from the Southwest Harbor Public Library Digital Archive (SWHPLDA). As the owner of Southwest Harbor's first automobile garage, Sim was the chief instigator of the area's "automobile war" when he was arrested for flaunting a ban on the newfangled machine in neighboring Bar Harbor.

In 1905, Sim bought shore property from the Clark family, put up a shop, built and repaired boats and installed naptha and gasoline engines. In 1912, he sold the property to Andrew Edward Parker, whose father, James, owned the fish wharf across the harbor that would become the Hinckley yard. Parker, "an excellent workman," established the Andrew Parker Boat Yard, with a repair shop and railway for craft up to thirty-five feet, a gas station and marine supplies, according to a 1921 *Country Living* magazine article by Alfred F. Loomis, via SWHPLDA. Parker was involved in civic affairs and pioneered the sale of internal combustion engines.

In 1925, Parker sold the business to Chester Eben Clement, who at forty-four was at the threshold of becoming a premier boatbuilder. Born in Monroe, Clement was twenty-one when he, Charles Perkins and Henry Kellam (a seaman with "a high standard of manhood") bought the Dirigo Boating Company in Bar Harbor, advertising a rental fleet of more than thirty sailboats, rowboats, launches and canoes to enjoy "the inspiration and grandeur" of the panorama, according to the *Bar Harbor Record*, via MDIHS.

Chester Clement. *Elaine Helbig Collection.*

Clement sold out after a few years. Ralph Stanley thinks that he may have next built boats at Sim Mayo's shop, also traveling to Cranberry Island to rebuild a sloop that went ashore in a storm.

In 1910, Chester married Grace Lunt, the daughter of sea captain Roland Lunt, from West Tremont. The two moved to Camden, where Chester worked for the Camden Anchor Rockland Machine Company, the largest anchor manufacturer in the country and producer of the Knox Gasolene Engine, according to the May 19, 1917 *Bar Harbor Record* and *History of Camden and Rockport, Maine* by Reuel Robinson.

When they returned to Southwest Harbor, Clement rented space to build boats and then bought Parker's yard. His work was renowned and the shop busy, keeping eight to ten employees active on everything from yachts to fishing boats "much admired by those who know the qualities of a seagoing boat," according to the *Bar Harbor Times* in 1927, via MDIHS.

Left: Grace (Lunt) Clement. *Elaine Helbig Collection.*

Below: Clement's *Princess Anne. W.H. Ballard photo/Elaine Helbig Collection.*

Clement's *Trailaway. Catherine Arlene Dolliver Spurling Collection/SWHPLDA.*

Clement's repertoire included a forty-foot charter boat with mahogany top and cabin, toilet and electric lights; a beautiful boat for Jacob Disston, president of the nation's largest handsaw manufacturer; a thirty-three-foot excursion boat; a thirty-footer of oak and cypress; and a thirty-one-footer for Raymond Bunker, who was still a young man out on Cranberry Isle. A fifty-foot, double-planked, mahogany-hull commuter boat designed by Eldredge-McInnis went to Richard Hart of Boston and Northeast Harbor. The boat was equipped with two Sterling-Petrel motors of 180 horsepower each, for a speed of twenty-five miles per hour. A twenty-five-foot mahogany-finish speedboat was destined for the lakes of New York. For Captain Francis Spurling, he built the lobsterboat *Trail Away.* According to Ralph Stanley, it took Clement only twenty-one days to build a fishing vessel for fisherman Harvard Beal.

"The Clement boats are gaining a widespread reputation as evinced by the number of orders, which increases every season. This industry means a good deal to Southwest Harbor, bringing employment and good wages to the place," reads a 1929 *Bar Harbor Times* article, via MDIHS.

The Clement boat *Wilderedge II*. *W.H. Ballard photo/Elaine Helbig Collection.*

During Prohibition, Clement built speedy boats. The forty-eight-foot, 360-horsepower *Pronto* and the fifty-five-foot, 580-horsepower *Pronto II* may have been rumrunners. The *Maybe*, eighty feet long with a sixteen-and-a-half-foot beam and three engines totaling 1,650 horsepower, was definitely a rumrunner, according to "Boatbuilding During World War II: MDI, Ellsworth, Stonington, and Blue Hill," by Ralph Stanley.

The *Maybe* "had armor plate by the steering section, and it had a little pilothouse that stuck up about a foot from deck, and little windows," Stanley said. "The boat left here on its way to New York, and the Coast Guard stopped it and inspected the papers. It was rated for fishing. Everything was in order, and they let it go. But they caught it on the first trip in with a load from offshore."

Many area boatbuilders started their careers with Clement, including Raymond Bunker. "Chester was quite a fellow," Bunker said in a 1974 interview recorded for the GHMM collection. "If he saw you were interested in your work, he was interested in you and helped you. Awfully nice man to work for. In fact, he was an awful nice man, period. He knew boatbuilding from A to Z. He built anything, from a ten-foot punt to a four-master. It didn't make a difference—it automatically came to him."

Raymond's brother Wilfred recalled, in a 1998 interview recorded for GHMM, that "Chester was one of those men that could look at a boat, get a plank and fix it in the right place without measuring anything, and Raymond learned to do that."

Clement died in a car accident in 1937 at fifty-six. He was on his way back home from Ellsworth after dropping a package in the mail. It was snowing pretty badly, and he went off the road by the bluffs near Echo Lake. "It's too bad because if he'd lived during World War II, I think he'd have done well," said Ralph Stanley.

Clement's son, Chester Harvard Clement, tried to keep the business going. But Clement's poor bookkeeping made it impossible to claim debts owed by owners who hadn't paid in full. Grace lost the house and eventually moved away. Chester H. had to sell the yard.

SARGENT WAS TWENTY-FOUR. With the help of his father, he purchased majority stock interest and named the yard the Southwest Boat Corporation. His father insisted that if he were going to put money into the enterprise, he wanted other businessmen in town to be involved as board members. "I think it just looked like a good business opportunity," David said. "Dad went to his father for financial support, and I think his father thought it might settle him down a little bit. Dad wanted to do something on his own."

Among Sargent's first projects, he worked on a design for a 38-foot motor cruiser and rebuilt the *George E. Klinck*, a three-masted, 152.6-foot lumber schooner built in 1904, which he found laid up in Rockland.

The *George E. Klinck*, seen here at a Rockland yard. *David Sargent Collection/SWHPLDA.*

BOATBUILDING ON MOUNT DESERT ISLAND

Business was about to boom. By 1941, it had become evident that the country would need a lot of small boats if the United States got into the war. Hinckley was in D.C., nailing down contracts, the first one for twenty 38-foot Coast Guard picket boats. Together, Hinckley and Sargent's two yards produced 535 war boats—mine yawls, tow yawls, aircraft personnel boats, picket boats and lifeboats—for the army, navy and Coast Guard. To cover the effort, the yards hired established boatbuilders as well as anyone else willing to learn. The yards ran two nine-hour shifts for more than two years. Before the government contracts, 34 men were on the payroll. By December 1942, more than 350 were employed at both yards, working for fifty to seventy-five cents per hour. New facilities were acquired—two sawmills, a lumberyard, two more marine railways, a derrick, a set of ways for boats up to 125 feet long, another joiner shop, another machine shop, a foundry, a pattern shop and nearly forty thousand square feet of covered floor space, according to Ben Hinckley's book.

According to Ralph Stanley, Hinckley's forward-thinking development of the production line made it possible to turn out boats rapidly. "One time, they were having a race, and the night crew planked up a whole boat in one night," Stanley said. "The day crew came the next day and had to take all the planks off and put them back again. They got going too fast."

There was a lot of drinking, too. "Down at Southwest Boat, they were working outdoors a lot, and they could drink all day long and not notice it out in that cold," Stanley said.

The two yards ultimately produced almost 40 percent of the state's total boat production for the armed services. They received the first combined Army-Navy E (excellence) ever conferred in Maine. Thurlow M. Gordon, a New York attorney, was master of ceremonies at a ceremony held outside Southwest Boat. "He spoke of the changed conditions that have brought mechanized warfare on an increasing scale and have made men in production, behind the guns, as much an integral part of the war effort as those in the front lines," a news report noted. "In former years, decorations were won in battle; now they are also won in shipyards and munitions plants."

DURING THE SAME PERIOD, Southwest Boat built large draggers, a sardine smack and a ferry. Among them was a sixty-foot dragger, *Sea Fox*, launched in 1942 for Manuel "Manny" Zora of Provincetown, Massachusetts. During Prohibition, Zora was a storied rumrunner. The Coast Guard nicknamed him the "Sea Fox."

The ninety-seven-foot dragger *Bonaventure*, built for brothers Nicholas and Joseph Novello, joined the redfish fleet at Gloucester, Massachusetts,

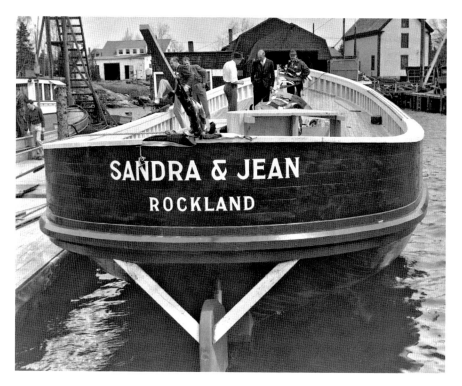

The dragger *Sandra & Jean*, under construction in the 1940s. *David Sargent Collection/SWHPLDA.*

after a period of war service. Bonaventure paid for itself quickly, but the job didn't profit Sargent. "He took the contract for $60,000, and it cost him $90,000 to build her," Stanley said. "I think all those boats he contracted, he lost money."

David agreed: "He was probably not a particularly good businessman, as he was far more interested in building boats than any of the chores of running a business, especially the financial aspects. He came to Southwest Harbor with a fair amount of money and left with none."

In the 1940s, Harvard Beal commissioned at least three more boats: the sardine carrier *Hornet*, the seiner *Lone Wolf* and the fishing boat *Ocean Belle*. That decade saw construction of at least a dozen other seiners, carriers, sportfishing boats and scallop draggers. The *Novelty*, a 64-foot sardine carrier homeported in Rockland, was still in use at least through the 1990s under the name *Lauren T*; it sank off the Rockland breakwater in 2007. Draggers launched every year or two—*Mary Rose* in 1942, *Cape Cod* in 1944, *Sandra & Jean* in 1945, *Connecticut* in 1946 and *Rhode Island*. In the 1950s, the yard

The *Connecticut. SWHPLDA.*

produced a 103-foot dragger with a 350,000-pound capacity, *Judith Lee Rose*, for Captain Frank Rose Jr., a Portuguese fisherman from Gloucester, to fish for redfish on the Grand Banks off Newfoundland. When redfish was fished out, by the late 1960s, the boat was a pioneer of the offshore lobster fishery, according to *White-Tipped Orange Masts: The Gloucester Dragger Fleet that Is No More*, by Peter Prybot, via SWHPLDA.

The big boats were too big for the old, antiquated shop, so they were built outdoors. David recalled, as a kid, seeing "the guys out there in woolen socks and rubber boots and several layers of clothing, standing in the snow and the weather." He also remembered gala boat launches. "When a big boat was launched, there was usually a large party. It seemed to me like half the town was there. The last one I remember was the *Judith Lee Rose*. We were just old enough, as young teenagers, to hang around and be a pain in the neck."

By 1956, at age thirteen, David also worked for his father. "At that time, the highest paid man in the shop was making about $1.10 an hour," he says. David earned $0.35 per hour. He went to his dad for a raise. "I said, 'Thirty-five cents an hour isn't much money.' He said, 'Well, you don't do much

The sardine carrier *Novelty* on launch day, 1944. *W.H. Ballard photo/SWHPLDA.*

Launching the cruiser *Thalia B*, 1938. *W.H. Ballard photo/SWHPLDA.*

The Southwest Boat buildings. *SWHPLDA.*

work.' I said, 'Well, I've got the experience now. I think I'm worth at least fifty cents.' He said, 'Listen, young man, I think you're costing me about a dollar and a half an hour to have you hang around here.' And that was the end of that."

Sargent was a complex person. Impatient and quick-tempered, he did not suffer fools gladly. He was also outspoken, generous and fun-loving. Ralph Stanley, a kid at the time, recalled some lore about Sargent's ways as a young man. "When he first got Southwest Boat, he was a single fellow, you know. He was kind of obsessed with Lincoln-Zephyr cars"—the latest, aerodynamic style debuted in 1936. "He stove up three of them, brand-new cars. One time, he come down over Carroll's Hill, went off the road, through an apple orchard, and ruined the car."

Another anecdote has it that Sargent and a friend were rescued, in hypothermia-inducing April, when they were found clinging to a gong buoy after their boat caught fire and burned out from under them. "The way Dad told this was it was a dead calm night on the Western Way," said David. "They were running speed trials on a Hickman Sea Sled [an inverted-V planing hull that debuted in 1913], a fast speedboat, belonging to Frank

Lyman. It was about midnight. The gas tank leaked, and the boat went up in flames. They managed to swim to, and get up onto, the gong buoy. They beat the gong, hoping someone would hear it. He said that after three or four hours, someone on Cranberry Island heard it and figured it shouldn't be ringing on such a calm night, so they called the Coast Guard."

David's summer job at the yard abruptly ended when he was nineteen. It was 1963. Sargent had sold controlling interest to John Briggs of Manset and headed off to Miami, Florida, to take a job as plant manager with the young but thriving Bertram Yacht, exploring designs and technologies for fiberglass powerboats. Left without a manager, Southwest Boat's board of directors hired Otto "Junior" Miller, active in Maine and New Brunswick's marine, fisheries and boating industries. Miller stayed with Southwest Boat through 1975 and then became director of boatbuilding at the Lubec campus of the Washington County Vocational Technical Institute. (He died unexpectedly in 1984 at fifty-nine.)

Business at Southwest Boat, in the early '60s, was tough, with wooden boat production nearly at a standstill. Sargent was interested in fiberglass, but he didn't have the large, moneyed, yachting customer base that Hinckley did to finance any changes. "I think Dad didn't get much satisfaction out of the storage and repair aspect of the business, and that is what Southwest Boat had become," David said.

When Bertram invited Sargent to manage his plant, he jumped at the chance. A year later, he formed Coburn and Sargent Inc. with Fred Coburn, designing and building custom fiberglass yachts, including the Aquasport 22, which would become a huge seller. When it became clear that the company was headed toward mass production, Sargent sold his interest to Coburn in order to focus on design. He drafted plans for a 115-foot, fiberglass version of the clipper ship *Cutty Sark*. This was followed by the design and construction of a 25-foot sportfisherman of the Aquasport type and the Purdue 18, an outboard sportfishing boat designed for bonefishing on Florida's saltwater flats.

By late 1967, he had partnered with Robert Schwebke, a Miami native, to form Mako Marine, manufacturer of outboard sportfishing boats. Sargent designed several Makos; by 1969, production was up to twenty boats per week. Thanks to Sargent's designs, Aquasport and Mako were two of the earliest companies (Boston Whaler was the first) to have the center console design now popular in the world of sportfishing boats.

Sargent took an adventurous turn when a friend introduced him to a man from Ecuador who built shrimp trawlers. "Dad had an idea to build some large motor yachts there because material and labor were so much less costly," David said. Sargent stayed in Ecuador much of the year to build wood trawler-yachts. His wife, Mary, visited several months at a time, and a partner in Miami marketed the boats. After five or six years, he returned to Mako for another ten or fifteen years, serving as chief designer. He died in 1989 at age seventy-three.

At one point, David was tempted to buy Southwest Boat, which was last up for sale in the early 1990s. (Audrey and Jeff Berzinis and Bonnie and Tom Sawyer purchased the yard and renamed it Southwest Boat Marine Services. In 1998, the Sawyers opted out, and it continues today with the Berzinises.) "I talked with a few friends, and we said we could gather up the money," David recalled. "But I started thinking about it, and I thought, 'Boy, I just don't have imagination enough to put together a business plan that would support that type of investment, even though I really wanted to do it.' Berzinis had much more imagination than I did."

Southwest Boat remains an important business in the area. For David, it represents a happy childhood. Living in a house at water's edge, David recalled swimming right off the beach; rowing and motoring around in one or another of the small boats available at the shop; the family cruises up Somes Sound to the pink ledges for picnics or out to their camp on Swan's Island; and the beauty of the wharf and pilings encased in ice, the harbor frozen, broken ice pancaked on the shore. "I had a pretty idyllic childhood," he said. "I describe it to other people, and they say 'Wow!' The boatshop was sort of our playground."

Chapter 11

FARNHAM BUTLER

A TASTE FOR CONTROVERSY

All the comments I had, I was about ready to take to the woods," Farnham Butler told a Great Harbor Maritime Museum interviewer in 2002, recalling the yachting world's reaction to his reverse-sheer design for a light-displacement sloop.

In 1950, Butler and a friend, naval architect Cyrus Hamlin, were trading sketches back and forth and doing experiments with lightweight, glued cedar-strip planking. Butler was the founder and owner of Mount Desert Yacht Yard, at the head of Somes Sound. In addition to storing and repairing boats, he was building tenders, prams and dinghies and had started into larger boats designed by his good friend John Alden and his brother-in-law, Ted Earl.

One day, a fellow named F.G. Grant, a neurosurgeon who summered in Pretty Marsh, came into Butler's office and wanted to buy a thirty-six-foot yawl. "I said, 'That boat meets absolutely none of your requirements,'" Butler recalled. "I pulled out a drawer and took out a bunch of drawings, some Cy's and some mine. I said, 'We can build a boat like that.'"

It was a radical design that helped spark a new approach to small auxiliaries. The sheer arched up amidships, a change that provided more room aboard and great stability and sea-kindliness. But it was startling to eyes accustomed to traditional sheerlines that were higher fore and aft. The use of glued-strip construction for boats was also new, made possible by the development of waterproof glues.

Grant named his sloop *Controversy*. Butler adopted the name for the model and patented the concept. In 1954, he rocked the yachting world again with

Farnham Butler. *Butler Family Collection.*

the invention of the Amphibi-Con, a boat trailerable by family car and the first to be sold in kit form to amateur builders. Butler's boats were popular far and wide, in a decade that would close with the decline of wooden boats and the surge of fiberglass.

Born in 1909, Butler loved to sail, loved being around boats in general and loved Maine.

Growing up in Morristown, New Jersey, his father, Arthur, was headmaster of the Morristown Boys School in New Jersey. His mother, Lydia, trained as a schoolteacher but likely spent her time fulfilling the social duties of a headmaster's wife, catering to a well-to-do clientele. The couple took their two boys, Farnham and Arthur Jr., to Southwest Harbor every summer and made it their permanent home in 1926 when Arthur retired; they built a house on the shore. The boys loved to fish, selling their catch door to door to neighbors. Farnham made his own sailboat with a sail made out of an old awning, stuck onto his rowboat.

Arthur Sr. had a Friendship sloop named *Euryale*, after one of the Gorgons of Greek mythology, and often took his sons cruising. In Morristown, a model of a Manchester 15 sat on the mantel, inspiring the boys to save their

An A boat sits on the back ways, circa 1930. *Butler Family Collection.*

pennies to buy their own. Around 1921, one of the prep school students caught pneumonia and stayed with the Butlers while he went through the crisis. The student's father wondered what he could do to repay the family's kindness, so he bought the boys their Manchester 15. The boys spent as much time on it as they could. As teenagers, they sailed A boats with the Northeast Harbor Fleet, where their father was vice-commodore. When Farnham was twenty, his father bought an Alden schooner and allowed his sons to participate in their first offshore race, to Bermuda.

Farnham was at Harvard at the time, majoring in economics. But he quit at the end of his junior year. "I was fed up with it," he said. "I decided I wanted to get into the boat business. Dad said, 'I want you to see my friend Charles Francis Adams,'" secretary of the navy under Hoover and a well-known yachtsman. "The first question he asked was, 'You got an independent income?' I said, 'Nope.' He said, 'You don't want anything to do with the boat business. You can't make a decent living.' We had a nice long talk. Finally, he said, 'I want you to see George Owen at MIT.' Owen is more or less the grandfather of yacht design. The question he asked was, 'Do you have an independent income?' I said, 'Nope.' He said, 'Why don't you try the shipyards?'"

Receiving a letter of introduction to the Bethlehem Shipbuilding Corporation, he got a job at its Quincy, Massachusetts shipyard, earning twelve dollars per week. "After a year and a half, I decided, if I had the general manager's job when I was forty, I wouldn't want it. So I went back to Harvard."

Graduating in 1933, he was unsuccessful getting a job with Herreshoff for anything it would pay, or even no pay at all. He knew he wanted to be in Maine, and he wanted to work at a boatyard. A fellow named Captain William H. Black, a talented racing professional who worked for a prominent Northeast Harbor family, had started a small yard at the head of Somes Sound in 1926. Farnham worked for Black for a few years. But it was the height of the Depression, and Black was beset by financial problems. In 1934, Farnham and his brother, backed by Dr. E.G. Stillman, a Seal Harbor summer resident, bought the yard and inherited an established clientele. Farnham also began building small craft for fun. His first commission was a rowboat. "I drew up plans and went and built her with Cliff Rich," he said. "The first boat Henry Hinckley ever built, too, was with Cliff Rich. Cliff was a wonderful fellow. When the day was over, his shop floor was so you could eat off it."

In 1937, Farnham met a young woman named Gladys Whitmore. The Whitmore family had been in Southwest Harbor since 1837. But Gladys's father, John, went off to Hawaii as a young man at the behest of Jim Dole, to help him found the eponymous pineapple company. Dole was looking for someone with canning experience, which John had, according to a 1989 interview recorded for MDIHS.

Gladys's mother, Edna, was the daughter of a Norwegian sea captain who sometimes brought his wife and daughter on his voyages to China and Australia. They often went to Hawaii. Edna would row ashore with her bicycle and pedal around to see her many friends. When she was eighteen or nineteen, she was in Honolulu and happened to meet John. The two got engaged by letter. She was voyaging back for her wedding when the boat was becalmed for forty days. "There was no communication, so my poor father would come through the muddy gulches, and there was no sign of the ship," Gladys said. Edna finally arrived and they married.

Gladys was born in 1918. The family occasionally made the arduous trip back to Southwest Harbor. Gladys remembered her first trip, at age six, arriving with her parents and sister by train in Boston, boarding the boat to Rockland and then getting on the steamer *J.T. Morse* to Southwest Harbor. "They loaded our stuff in an old horse and wagon, and we went up the hill, and as we drove in, I had never seen wildflowers in such abundance," she said. "It seemed like a magical world."

She was fifteen when her father died from a gall bladder infection. Her two older siblings had moved east, and her mother returned to the Whitmore house in Southwest Harbor. Gladys stayed in Hawaii another year to finish

The forty-four-foot navy yawl *Swift. Butler Family Collection.*

high school and then moved east to attend Smith College. Edna was trying to figure out how to get her daughter to come to Southwest Harbor for the summer. Gladys said that she'd come home if she could buy a boat. Edna agreed to $100. Gladys cased the boatyards and met Farnham, who found her a $75 O boat and proceeded to hang around, offering his expert advice. He wanted to marry right off, but Gladys made him wait until she graduated, in 1938. They built the home next to the yard in 1940 and had their first child a year later.

Farnham bought a strip of land in Northeast Harbor to build a marine railway, chandlery and offices. Gladys worked there while Farnham ran the main yard and built boats. During World War II, like Hinckley and Southwest Boat, he took on navy contracts, eventually building twenty-five thirty-eight-foot buoy boats, three forty-four-foot yawls and ninety fifteen-foot workboats. Farnham helped form the Maine Boat Builders Association, which built four seventy-two-foot launches for lend-lease to Britain.

The workboats were lightly built. Farnham couldn't make out what was going on until a woman nearby called to say her son had landed on a Pacific island and noticed the nameplate on the stern, Mount Desert Yacht Yard, before leaving the boat behind. That's when Farnham realized that they were throwaway boats, getting troops into places where landing craft couldn't go. "I always say I spent the war fighting the navy, because dealing with the navy was next to impossible," Farnham said. "I gather, from what Henry Hinckley said, the army was easier to deal with because the army didn't know what they were talking about anyway."

After the war, the yard readjusted. Farnham had designed the thirty-seven-foot Maine Coast Yawl and built the first, *Snowflake*, for his family in 1945, followed by two sister ships and a thirty-five-foot sloop named *Scandal*. But boatbuilding was financially unrewarding at the time; boats were sold for about as much as it cost to build them. So Farnham returned to smaller craft—numerous tenders, a fleet of Charles Mower–designed eighteen-foot catboats called Massachusetts Bay Hustlers and twenty-three-foot knockabouts designed by Butler and Earl that they called Mermaids. Farnham undertook improvements at the Northeast Harbor yard to make it attractive to yachters, with little luck. The 1940s ended with some discouragement. But his interest was piqued by developments in lighter-displacement boats taking place in England.

"I was much intrigued with the idea as a means of reducing the cost of building cruising boats," he wrote in a short history of the yard. "Cy Hamlin was following a somewhat similar approach, and in 1951 the yard built a 29-foot sloop, the *Kittiwake*, from his designs. I was not happy with this design and began working with Hamlin on plans for a somewhat similar yet radically different boat." That developed into the first Controversy. The Controversy 26 was developed around the same time, followed by the Controversy 36.

In 1954, Farnham was approached by Chuck Angle, a boat designer and sailor from Rochester, New York. Chuck was looking for a family cruising boat that could be loaded on a trailer and towed behind a station wagon. Farnham and Cy Hamlin designed a twenty-five-foot, glue-stripped sloop, sea-kindly and easy to build, and called it the Amphibi-Con. Farnham then took patterns from Chuck's boat. He made the patterns and kit setups available to the public, so that nonprofessionals, as well as other professionals, could build their own boats. Amateurs had a blast, and the Amphibi-Con would become the yard's most popular boat.

"I had a chap who was a Montana wheat farmer," Farnham recalled. "He ordered a setup kit. That was the bulkheads, the deck on, the house sides on, but no planking. He wanted to pick it up the first of December and go south with her. He called and had to cancel. He said, 'We've had a

Controversy 36 No. 1, *Constellation*, 1953. *W.H. Ballard photo/Butler Family Collection.*

Amphibi-Con No. 1, *QED*, 1954. *Butler Family Collection.*

Controversy 27 No. 1, *Rubicon*, 1960, with Betsy, Lydia and Gladys at the helm. *W.H. Ballard photo/Butler Family Collection.*

blizzard, and we'll never be able to get south.' I said, 'I guarantee, if you can get to Chicago, you can get from here south.'" The farmer picked up the boat, drove to Florida and set up in a boatyard. "The first thing he did was build the bunks, put a canvas over her and move aboard. Then they started planking. He took that boat from the south back up to Montana, worked on it between planting and harvest, took her south again and, before the winter was out, launched her. He had never built a boat before in his life."

Owners ranged far and wide. "Gil Houston and his wife, Ruth, have just completed the long trip from Chicago to Florida in their A/C Cloud 9," Farnham wrote in a 1961 newsletter. "They trailed to Washington and thence went down the Inland Waterway. Gil writes, 'By the time we are through we will have traveled with Cloud 9 about 1,500 miles on water and well over 2,000 miles by trailer on this one trip. With previous trips, we should soon be approaching the 7,500-mile mark.'"

Over the next few years, Butler and Hamlin, and then Earl, designed several custom yachts, the twenty-four-foot Amphibi-ette and two new

Controversies, the 27 and 28. But the emergence of fiberglass and competition from foreign imports quashed new construction. In 1962, the yard built its last boat. "For us, the production of small boats far from the large markets was uneconomic; imported boats could be delivered near the markets at prices far below our costs," Farnham wrote. "Many of our designs were, therefore, commissioned abroad, with boats being built in England, Holland, Denmark, Norway, and Finland. Plans were also provided for construction in Japan, Yugoslavia, South Africa, British Colombia, and elsewhere."

With Gladys helping out, and four children coming on through the years to pump boats, run errands and crew, the yard became a family affair. Lydia Butler Goetze remembered growing up there as a wonderful experience. There were lots of little boats around, and the kids were allowed to grab them anytime. "I remember the first day I was allowed to sail a little catboat all by myself," she said. "I was four years old. It was a calm summer morning, and I was allowed to go out by myself. My mom sat on the float. When it was time for me to come back, she gave me directions on how to do that."

Still, continual pressure and little time off left Farnham exhausted. In the 1960s, he began to let things slide. One of the buildings collapsed in a blizzard, and others were in disrepair. Three of the children moved on to

Scandal under construction. *Butler Family Collection.*

other endeavors, and Farnham thought about closing the yard. But he held on to see if his youngest, John, would take over. When John graduated from college, in 1971, he did just that. He was soon rebuilding and modernizing both yards, by 1985 leaving only Bill Black's original shack. Farnham helped John plan the reconstructions, arguing along the way, and John made a nice, steady business that's today a mainstay for multiple generations of customers.

Farnham and Gladys sailed as much as possible, played tennis and ping-pong, skied, skated, swam and remained active in civic affairs. Farnham was still sailing in his nineties. "Is there any project you'd single out that was especially satisfying?" an interviewer asked in 2002. "Oh, gosh," replied Farnham, "They've all been satisfying!"

Chapter 12

NOBODY BUILT THEM LIKE SIM DAVIS

There's a great old building on the Bass Harbor shore. In recent decades, it was used by a few boatyards to store spars. But it goes back at least to the early 1900s, when it was part of a larger complex called the McKinley Fish & Freezer Company, a cold storage plant.

In between fish and spars, Grandville "Sim" Davis was there building boats. He left telltales. A friend of mine who worked for Morris Yachts, the yard's owner up to 2015, took me for a tour—the building was sturdy, its bits tattered and salty. Sim's ghostly presence starts outside on the sawed-back ways under the building, moves to the cavernous first floor that once housed large vessels under construction, takes you up narrow stairs to Sim's steambox on an upper balcony and then up more stairs to the attic.

"Watch out. Many a person has gotten clobbered," Bruce said, warning me against a low beam. A bit of light filters through a few windows. Adjusting to the dark, I notice a complex of curves and straight lines penciled on the worn wood floor. This was where Sim lofted his designs; the lines here represent his last boat. "Here's the centerline," he said, walking the far-flung length of the floor. "Here's the first station. This is the stem down here. This straight line is probably the base line." We creep through the gloom, finding numbers for each station. "This was a huge boat, probably the biggest thing he ever built. The shop won't take any bigger. They were here on their hands and knees, laying this stuff out."

Sim's nephew, Bob Davis, remembered heading up the crew to build that last boat. It was the early 1970s. Sim was in his eighth decade and

Above: McKinley Fish and Freezer. *Michael Dawes Collection.*

Left: Sim Davis. *Michael Dawes Collection.*

increasingly troubled by arthritis, but he had taken a job to design and build a sixty-foot party fishing boat for a New Jersey customer. Sim was meticulous; Bob followed his directions closely. "His workmanship was good in everything he did. He was very fussy," he said. "He had a unique way of putting in the shaft log. He would want that dovetailed into the keel. You're handling a two-hundred-pound piece of oak. I don't know how many times I put that all the way down and back. You had to set it just like it was glued there. I'm not sure dovetailing is any better, but if you find a boat with that piece dovetailed into the keel, it's Sim's boat."

Sim's grandson, Michael Dawes, also worked here a while. Mike recalled measuring and cutting the planks to fit each other exactly. "You had to keep adjusting so it looked good when it was done. And when each plank went in, you had to plane a caulking seam in it, and so on," he said. "Gramps never had geometry. He just knew what it should look like. He had an eye and a knack for it, and that came from years of experience."

SIM WAS BORN IN 1897 on Frenchboro, a small island nine miles off Bass Harbor. His roots on Frenchboro and Swan's Island go back to the early 1800s. His grandfather, Captain William Davis, was a fisherman. His father, Leaman Davis, built boats and operated one of the first island businesses dedicated to buying lobsters, selling them to a Portland dealer, according to *Hauling by Hand: The Life and Times of a Maine Island* by Dean Lawrence Lunt.

Sim was one of nine children. He likely learned boatbuilding from his father; two brothers, Ben Davis Sr. and Elmer "Goog" Davis, also built boats. When he was twenty-one, Sim married Violet Thurlow, another Frenchboro native. It was apparently a shotgun wedding, as several months after the wedding, they had their first child, Theda. Their daughter June came along a year later, followed by Marilyn, who died at age eight. Thelma was the baby.

Times were tough. June lived with her grandmother most of the time because Sim and Violet couldn't afford all the kids. In Lunt's book, June recalled that her grandmother made all her clothes, even her underpants. The children went barefoot in the summer so they wouldn't wear out their shoes. But she and Theda had plenty of fun. "We went berrying up in the woods. We had playhouses all over the place," she said in the Lunt book. "There was a great tree with a swing, and under it was rock and that rock was a playhouse."

June was young when the family moved to Bass Harbor. Called McKinley at the time, it was a village of fishermen, boatbuilders and people who worked at the Underwood sardine-packing plant, getting paid two cents per can. When the herring boats came in, the factory whistle blew to signal packers to come down. June was the fastest packer. But even then, no one was getting rich.

The family's home was near the shop; there was a set of rustic cabins out back. Violet worked at the plant, handled the books for her husband's company and took care of the cabins, rented seasonally. She'd cuss about the salt spray on the windows. "Danged house, so near the water!" Mike recalled her saying.

Sim was active in civic affairs, helping establish ferry service between his wharf and Frenchboro and Swan's Island and investing in the Southwest Boat Corporation, where he worked a short time. Mostly, though, he was on his own, partly because he was a tough old bird, cussing and losing his temper, and nobody liked to work with him. "He was kind of grumpy. He wanted it his way," Mike said. "But he built stuff to last."

A short fellow, perhaps five-foot-six, he cleaned up well, grew stout with age and liked to joke. In his retirement, he would recite poetry and sing songs or "blither away," as Mike said, on his CB. The FCC once fined him. "My grandmother was so embarrassed," Mike said. "He was a real character."

He worked nonstop. A friend from Frenchboro who also moved to McKinley, Carroll Lunt, would one day have Sim build a boat for him. "Long before daylight, in the winter, no matter how cold, he'd go right down and go to work," Carroll recalled. The building was uninsulated, with only a wood stove to heat the cavernous space. "There'd be no fire until someone came down to build one. He'd say, 'Gosh, it's cold in here.' And he'd keep right on working."

"He would just come up for meals," Mike said. "He drove himself hard as hell, working into the night, then crawling into bed. It was a tough living."

It was a thriving business in the 1940s and early '50s. Known for his rugged construction, Sim built two or three boats every year. "Gramps had a Cadillac. Father said that meant he had arrived," Mike laughed. Muriel Davisson knows that it was 1941 when Sim built the *Esther I*, a classy lobsterboat that her father designed for fishing and charter parties. Her mother was varnishing the cabin, and Muriel was born that night. "Must have been the fumes," she laughed.

In 1947 or '48, Sim built a lobsterboat for Alton Mitchell, the father of Muriel's childhood friend Theolyn Gilley. "He built quite a few boats in the harbor here," said Theolyn. "I spent half my life on that boat." From a young age, Alton gently woke his daughter before dawn, fed her breakfast, helped her into her little black and red boots and headed down to the boat,

J.L. Stanley & Sons. Tremont Historical Society.

tying her in so she wouldn't fall overboard. "I stayed out all day and helped him fish. I adored my father."

Around the same time, Sim launched the fifty-eight-foot dragger *J.L. Stanley & Sons*, flags flying bow to stern. The dragger was towed from Bass Harbor to Southwest Harbor for rigging, greeted by whistles and bells. Built for the Stanley Fish and Lobster Company in Manset, the occasion was marked by praise for Captain Stanley's vision as a pioneer in the fish business, "his foresight and business acumen and the judgment with which he managed the firm until his death at past 80," according to a THS newsletter. Manset was the area's center of fishing, and Stanley's concern, started in 1874, covered much of the waterfront, employing many people at its fish wharf, ice harvesting business and cold storage plant. The wharf was also used as a steamboat landing. Fire destroyed the concern, and other waterfront businesses, in 1918, but Stanley rebuilt. The business was destroyed by fire again in 1967, according to the SWHPLDA.

The sixty-two-foot, nine-inch dragger *Dorothy and Betty II*, destined for Stonington, was "thoroughly equipped with modern gear and finished in

Lawrence Wayne. Michael Dawes Collection.

brightened cypress." The forty-one-foot *Golden Eagle* was a pleasure boat for a Brooksville summer family; it had "special screening over the portholes and other windows" and "a handsome figurehead of a flying golden eagle trailing golden stars from its taloned feet," according to an unidentified news clipping via THS.

Soon after came the fifty-two-foot *Gary Alan* and fifty-four-foot *Lawrence Wayne*, both herring carriers, for sardine-packing plants in Jonesport and Milbridge. The ships joined a fleet up of more than ninety carriers that bailed herring out of the stop-seines and transported them to packing plants then prevalent in most Maine coastal towns, according to *Sardine Carriers and Seiners of the Maine Coast*, compiled and written by Paul E. Bennett, via SWHPLDA.

Sim was well known by the Massachusetts fishing fleet. He built a dragger named *Liberty Belle* for Henry Passion and another dragger, *CR&M*, for Ferdinand "Ferdy" Salvador.

One of the most respected fishermen in Provincetown was Manuel Thomas, a hardworking skipper and top moneymaker. Genially known as "Doctor Foo" or "Doc," for his childhood enthusiasm for Charlie Chan and the Doctor Foo Man Chu series, Manuel, born in Fuzeta, Portugal,

Liberty Belle. Tremont Historical Society.

was young when his family moved to Gloucester. His father, Louis, ran a dragger there, as well as later in Provincetown. Manuel began fishing with his father at age sixteen in the early 1920s. Once, while checking the engine, Manuel was overcome by fumes from a leaky exhaust pipe. His younger brother, Joe, dragged him into the fresh air and applied artificial respiration. To make matters worse, Louis suffered a heart attack. Both men survived. Another time, when the boat was tied alongside Sklaroff's Wharf during a southwester, Manuel threw some twine aboard the boat, got his fingers tangled in the meshes and went overboard. The only thing injured was his pride, according to the article "Meet Our Fishing Fleet" by Jack Rivers Jr., via Salvador Vasques.

Manuel loved the lines of Sim's draggers, particularly the *St. Peter III* in Gloucester and *Liberty Belle*, whose owner was a relative (and *CR&M*'s owner was his son Tom's godfather). But he wanted his boat heavier, wider and longer than *Liberty Belle*. (Over the years, *Liberty Belle* was rammed twice, sunk twice and raised twice, hit first in the fog by a ferry and next by a fishing boat.) Sim redesigned the hull, made it three feet longer, a foot wider and

CR&M at Southwest Boat. *W.H. Ballard photo/SWHPLDA.*

maybe a foot deeper. "That boat was one of the most rugged boats around," said Tom, who was five in 1949 when he and his family traveled to Sim's shop for the dragger's launch.

The family stayed in one of Sim and Violet's rental cottages. "I remember he reminded me of my father," Tom said. "He was bald, just a bit of hair. He was very nice, always smiling. The guy was never without a smile."

Tom and his mother christened the dragger, named after him and his sister. The *Joan & Tom*, at sixty-two feet nine inches and able to carry sixty thousand pounds of fish, was pronounced one of the best in the fleet. Accommodations were "princely," with a complete pantry and cooking arrangements, freshwater tank and fishing gear. "Despite her large carrying capacity, she still has slender and graceful lines," according to an unidentified news clipping via THS.

Starting at age ten, Tom fished fourteen years with his father, going after haddock, cod and flounder, as well as "trash fish" such as whiting and hake, used to feed the minks that became coats. In 1968, off Chatham, the boat

Joan & Tom. Salvador Vasques Collection.

hit a submerged object and sank. "Our lights went out. My father told me to go to the engine room and see what's wrong. Water was up to the batteries. Whatever it was stove a hole. We only felt a little thud." The boat sank in eighty feet of water in ten minutes, just enough time for the crew—Tom, his father and three uncles—to get their dory into the water. With a dozen fishing boats in the area, they were in no danger while they waited for the Coast Guard to pick them up.

Another Sim Davis aficionado, Mickey Varians from Sebago, Maine, raised the boat. "It was a feat. They said he'd never do it." Varians fixed it and went shrimping for five years and then sold it. The *Joan & Tom* went to Boston for a few years, returned to P-town and was cut up in 2005. But before it was, Tom asked the owner if he would look for a silver dollar his father had placed under the mast for good luck. "My wedding ring is made out of that silver dollar, and with the silver left over, I had a charm made for my daughter, who had cancer. She's eight years in remission now."

In 1964, Carroll Lunt had Sim build him a new lobsterboat. He visited the shop every day, admiring Sim's meticulous craftsmanship. "The seams were just so tight, when he put the caulking in. It didn't have any leaks. Sim would leave his planks outdoors, and he'd get them with frost in them, and fit them in the boat, and as the frost came out, they expanded a little and made the seams tighter. That was one of his secrets. And the way he put the wood together at the bottom of the boat—it was all built in, the hornbeam and sternpost and everything was all dovetailed together. It would stay there even without fastenings. Of course, they did fasten it. He used real heavy fastenings." Many years later, Carroll took the boat to Chummy Rich for new fastenings and caulk. "Chummy, a very good boatbuilder himself, growled about Sim having the seams so tight it was hard to get the caulking in." Carroll had the boat into the 2000s. It's still around. Somebody painted the top purple.

In those later years, Sim got scammed building a pleasure boat for well-to-do New York fellows. He took his payment by thirds, with the last third coming upon completion. "The boat was done, and they come up and look at it," Mike said. "It was out on a mooring. He got up the next morning, and the boat was gone. They just jumped on the boat and took off south. As soon as they crossed the Maine line, it was pretty tough for Gramps to recover it. There were no serial numbers or anything to title a boat in them days. The remaining third, which was a sizeable chunk of change, he didn't get that."

Bob recalled, "He said he should have suspected something when he showed up with an old beat-up Nash when he previously came with a Cadillac."

Toward the end, Sim was pretty lame. "He had a lot of arthritis," Mike recalled. "Hunkering over keels, chiseling away, the dead of winter, wind blowing in under there. He didn't seal up the shop to the outside air very well, so the tide would go out and the wind would blow in. The wood stove was way up at the head, so when he'd become numb enough, he'd go and warm up, then go do some more. He'd drag himself home for lunch, then back down he'd go. He'd just keep at it and keep at it."

In 1971, Sim sold the yard to Bob and Tina Hinckley, who started a service operation that became part of the Hinckley Company. Sim stayed on at the house until his death in 1979 at age eighty-one. He spent his last years puttering around, adding onto the house, playing guitar and singing songs on the CB. "Nobody built them like Sim Davis," Carroll said. "He spent lots of hours that he almost didn't get paid for. He didn't count his hours. There are good boatbuilders here. But I just think he was the best."

EPILOGUE

I just think he was the best." I bet any fan of any builder here would say the same thing. And there are others: Norman Bouchard in Southwest Harbor, Merton and James Rich in Bernard, John Cochran in Hulls Cove.

Bion Farnsworth, a fourth-generation builder from near Jonesport, moved to Hulls Cove and built powerboats, sailboats, dinghies, dories and punts, with his son Buddy eventually joining him. They built the Islesford ferry, a miniature tug and fishing boats. During the "herring craze," Bion built ninety-eight fishermen's dories in three years. Single-handed, Buddy built two punts in two days, throwing up a tarpaper shack under which to work when it began to rain. When Bion moved to MDI, most fishing boats were double-enders. He squared off the stern from the start for greater stability. This was an innovation. "They looked pretty funny to people then," chuckled Bion, when interviewed for an April 1, 1961 article by LaRue Spiker in the *Lewiston Evening Journal*. "They started calling them wood boxes because of the flat stern."

In 1946, Eugene "Gene" Walls, recently returned from the war, visited his distant cousin-in-law Bobby Rich. "He said, 'You know how to paint?'" Walls chuckled. "I said, 'Yeah, I know how to paint.' He said, 'We need a painter.'"

Walls, with zero boatbuilding experience, started low and rose high. During his twenty-one years there, he worked on more than one hundred boats, eventually mentoring Bobby's son Chummy. In 1967, Walls went into business for himself, building boats and houses.

Chummy said that he learned a lot from his father and grandfather. "But the actual person who was right by my side, who taught me all the little tricks, was Gene Walls."

In 1950, Lyford Stanley, in Bass Harbor, built his first boat in his bedroom. Soon he built a proper shop and numerous wooden lobsterboats. His wife, Norma, got a job in Hinckley's fiberglass shop, run by John "Jock" Williams. Norma convinced Jock that the fishing boat industry was going to move from wood to glass. Lyford's models would make great plugs for building fiberglass fishing boats, she said. Jock wanted to go into business for himself. So, in 1973, Jock; his wife, Deb; and Norma pulled a mold off the thirty-six-footer that Lyford was building. It was the beginning of a long partnership and friendship. Jock launched scores of Stanley 36s and built many other Stanleys in various sizes. Lyford worked at Jock's shop on the finish. He also fished, drove a water taxi and excursion boat, carpentered, ran movies, managed a band, did his own wiring and plumbing, had a sawmill, offered haircuts to elderly shut-ins, was a crack shot and made a pretty damned

Lyford Stanley (left) and Jock Williams. *John M. Williams Collection.*

good-looking set of false teeth. Later, he got into computers and played online poker. If you were on a boat in the fog, you wanted to be with Lyford. "He had fun. He'd terrorize us a little bit," said Jock.

In 1998, Lyford was inducted into the Maine Boat Builders Hall of Fame. "Lyford was an authentic, traditional Maine boatbuilder," said Jock, interviewed with Lyford's daughter Roxanne Lewis and others on February 4, 2009, for the MDIHS.

In the 1970s, a slew of fiberglass boat builders started in, while small wood builders hung on. Tom Morris arrived in Southwest Harbor from Philadelphia to finish glass Friendship sloops produced by Jarvis Newman and then teamed up with designer Chuck Paine to build classic sailboats and high-end performance cruisers. Tom bought the old Sim Davis yard (recently sold) and later Able Marine. After his son Cuyler joined the company, the two continued through the 2000s building modern Sparkman & Stephens–designed daysailers.

Lee Wilbur opened a one-bay shop in Seawall, finished Newman's hulls and then built a new plant in Manset. Ralph Ellis designed some models for Lee, who also finished hulls from other manufacturers. Today, Lee's daughter, Ingrid, and son-in-law, John Kachmar, own the business. "Ralph was soft-spoken and one of the hardest-working men I've ever known," Lee wrote in a 2010 article for Fishermen's Voice. "Kind, honest as the day was long, there was nothing he wouldn't do for a neighbor or friend. Just across the street was another boatbuilder and superb craftsman, Fairfield Morse. Fairfield left me and our boat yard with this simple statement: 'If it isn't right, then it isn't right.'"

Crozier Fox started Able Marine in his garage in Southwest Harbor. The stern of the boat touched the rear wall, and the bow was six inches from the door. To plane a plank, he cut a hole in the door and fed the board through. He later moved operations to Trenton to build high-end custom yachts.

Mac and Alice Pettegrow started Malcolm L. Pettegrow Inc. to build custom cold-molded yachts—from Downeast lobsterboats to fast sportfishermen—later building in fiberglass, too. Their son Al carries on today. Vic Levesque in Hulls Cove built big steel vessels. Ty Proctor in Bar Harbor, Robert Lincoln of Pretty Marsh, Ed Davis of Seal Cove and Davis Irvin of West Tremont built small wooden boats.

Through the years, add to the mix Weldon "Bunny" Leonard at Mount Desert Island Boatworks; Eric Clark, who hung his shingle as Marine Systems; David Schlaefer, building Mitchell Cove boats in Bernard; and Steve "Peach" Frederick in Bernard, his shop later occupied by Anthony

Fernandez and, lately, by Carlton Johnson, who learned fiberglass from Jock Williams in the early 1980s and now builds classic launches as Redfern Boats. (In 1999, Carlton bought the original Bobby Rich waterfront to set up as Up Harbor Marine.) John Brooks in Town Hill and Barry Buchanan in Bass Harbor built small wood boats, and Jean Beaulieu started Classic Boat Shop in Bernard to build cold-molded wood daysailers, later offering fiberglass, and continuing today.

I RETURNED TO THE Tremont Historical Society in search of an old Sim Davis photo and couldn't resist again poring over the collection's binders full of documents. A sentence caught my eye: "The last boat he built was the Myra J. Wooster, in Bass Harbor, in 1918."

Wait, 1918? I felt a lack of completion coming on. I homed in on the February 1947 article by E.M. Holmes, in an unidentified publication, and read about Joseph E. Wooster, who operated a farm in Warren, built two scallop draggers there, taught school, made clam and sardine cans and bossed the canning factories for thirteen years. Then he moved to Bernard, where he built the *Myra J. Wooster*, a sixty-three-foot sailing vessel that carried salt fish to Gloucester and freight between Belfast and Bass Harbor. When the article was written, he had been in house carpentry and contracting for twenty-seven years when he suddenly laid the keel for a twenty-two-foot sloop.

"The building was so small that Joe was obliged to extend it to accommodate the stern, and the sloop's eight-foot beam was so close to the inside measurements of the shed that no attempt was made to nail some of the planks to the timbers amidships until the otherwise completed hull had moved into the open. Joe built the boat for his own pleasure and use, but admits he will sell practically anything if somebody offers the right price."

Immediately, I dug into the Internet to search for old Joe's descendants. And there they are: Eva, who married Ralph and had Rosamund, Prudence and Marilyn. Prudence, who had Sam and…And so it continues—albums in attics, portraits in sheds, newspapers in morgues, letters in shoeboxes. Nowadays, add to that digital remains behind passwords. All neatly stowed, awaiting our inquiring eyes.

BIBLIOGRAPHY

Bennett, Paul E. *Sardine Carriers and Seiners of the Maine Coast*. Freeport, ME: Bennett Engineering, 1991.

Blanchard, Peter P., III. *We Were an Island: The Maine Life of Art and Nan Kellam*. N.p.: UPNE, 2010.

Boating. "TV Star's Tugboat" (February 1962). Available courtesy of the Robert "Chummy" Rich Collection.

Bray, Maynard. "Maddy Sue: An Early Picnic Boat." *WoodenBoat*, no. 222 (2011).

Digital Newspaper Archives of Friends of Island History, via Mount Desert Island Historical Society. islandhistory.newspaperarchive.com.

Duncan, Roger. *Dorothy Elizabeth: Building a Traditional Wooden Schooner*. N.p.: W.W. Norton & Company, 2000.

Ellsworth American. "Boat-Building Company Formed in S.W. Harbor." January 15, 1947.

Field, Rachel. *God's Pocket: The Story of Captain Samuel Hadlock Junior of Cranberry Isles*. Maine: Macmillan, 1934.

BIBLIOGRAPHY

Hamlin, Talbot, with Jessica Hamlin, colorist. *We Took to Cruising, from Maine to Florida Afloat*. N.p.: Sheridan House, 1951.

Hinckley, Benjamin Barrett, Jr., with Nancy W. McKelvy, illustrator. *The Hinckley Story*. N.p.: Pilot PR Inc., 1997.

Lauderdale, David. "Little Toot's Journey." *Island Packet*, December 1, 2003. lowcountrynewspapers.net/archive/node/94229.

Lunt, Dean Lawrence. *Hauling by Hand: The Life and Times of a Maine Island*. N.p.: Islandport Press, 1999.

Merkel, Jeanne St. Andre. *Nine Boats and Nine Kids: A True Chronicle*. N.p.: Ledge Books, 1984.

Milner, Craig, and Ralph Stanley. *Ralph Stanley: Tales of a Maine Boatbuilder*. N.p.: Down East Books, 2004.

Newman, Eleanor. "Three Boatyards Vital Industry to Southwest Harbor Community." Unidentified publication, May 17, 1948. Available courtesy of the Newman Family Collection.

Plimoth Plantation. "Mayflower II FAQs." https://www.plimoth.org/what-see-do/mayflower-ii/mayflower-ii-faqs.

Prybot, Peter. *White-Tipped Orange Masts: The Gloucester Dragger Fleet that Is No More*. Charleston, SC: The History Press, 2007.

Ralph Stanley: An Eye for Wood. Video documentary. Dobbs Productions, Bar Harbor, ME, 2015.

Shepard, Oscar. "Emblem of Honor at Southwest Harbor." Unidentified news publication. Available courtesy of the Mary Anne (Hinckley) Mead Collection.

Shettleworth, Earle G., Jr., and Lydia B. Vandenbergh. *Mount Desert Island: Somesville, Southwest Harbor, and Northeast Harbor*. Charleston, SC: Arcadia Publishing, 2001.

Spiker, LaRue. "The Sea Holds Strange Fascination for the Farnsworth Family." *Lewiston Evening Journal*, April 1, 1961.

Stanley, Ralph W. "Boatbuilding During World War II: MDI, Ellsworth, Stonington and Blue Hill." Private document.

Stelmok, Jerry. "A Mentor Would Appear: Mick Fahey and the North Woods Way." *WoodenBoat* (1985).

Thornton, Mrs. Seth S. "Nell." In *Traditions and Records of Southwest Harbor and Somesville*. N.p.: Merrill & Webber Company, 1938.

Unidentified publication. "Expert Boat Builders Are These Maine Boys." 1927/28.

Working Waterfront. "Sunken Sardine Carrier Going Nowhere." October 1, 2008.

Wurmfeld, Hope Herman. *Boatbuilder*. N.p.: Atheneum, 1988.

INDEX

Visit us at
www.historypress.net

· ·

This title is also available as an e-book